P9-BZY-418

the Economics of Macro Issues

Fourth Edition

Cover cartoon drawn by Dean Vietor.

Cover design by the Taly Design Group, Minnetonka, MN.

Library of Congress Cataloging in Publication Data

Miller, Roger LeRoy.
    The economics of macro issues.
    Includes index.
    1. Macroeconomics.   I.   Title.
HB172.5.M53 1983   339   82-13642
ISBN 0-314-69667-9

1st Reprint—1983

the Economics of Macro Issues

Fourth Edition

ROGER LeROY MILLER

Professor of Economics
School of Business
and
Law & Economics Center
University of Miami

WEST PUBLISHING COMPANY

St. Paul   New York   Los Angeles   San Francisco

Contents

v

3

4

5

Part Two

6

7

8

9

10

11

Part Three

The Keynesian Model, Fiscal Policy, and the Public Debt   65

12

Are We Saving Enough?   67

13

Social Security and Saving   70

14

Can the Government Create Jobs Directly?   76

15

The New Federalism and Automatic Stabilizers   82

16

17

18

Part four

19

20

2I

22

23

Part five

24

25

Part Six

26

27

28

29

Part Seven

30

31

Preface

Macroeconomic issues continue to dominate political discussions and news stories. The major issues of the day are inflation, disinflation, unemployment, high interest rates, and low economic growth. Taxes have remained a major political football. Unprecedented federal budget deficits have prompted a renewed interest in a constitutional amendment to balance the budget. This edition of *The Economics of Macro Issues* addresses itself to these problems and more.

The Economics of Macro Issues is a companion volume to *The Economics of Public Issues* which I co-authored with Douglass C. North. The objectives of both books are the same, except that the issues treated here correspond to the macro part of a standard economics principles course. The short chapters in this book should not be considered complete in any sense; rather the bare economic bones of some aspects of the issues treated are exposed. The issues are written to elicit additional discussion of the topics under study and to raise points generally not found in a principles text. Indeed, some of the arguments presented are intended to be controversial so that the student may be more inclined to participate in discussions of the issues.

New Chapters

Twelve new chapters have been added to this book. They are:

Chapter 1 *A Constitutional Amendment to Balance the Federal Budget*

Chapter 4 *The 18% Solution—Loopholes Beware*

Chapter 12 *Are We Saving Enough?*

Chapter 14 *Can the Government Create Jobs Directly?*

Chapter 15 *The New Federalism and Automatic Stabilizers*

Chapter 17 *The Deficit, Off-Budget Items, and Credit Markets*

Chapter 18 *The Full Employment Budget Rides Again*

Chapter 22 *Resolved: The U.S. Treasury Shall Issue Indexed Bonds*

Chapter 23 *The Costs and Benefits of Inflation*

Chapter 25 *Deposit Insurance and Bank Risk Taking*

Chapter 29 *Can Supply Side Economics Work?*

Chapter 30 *The Cost of Trade Restrictions*

Pedagogical Improvements

Numerous adopters of previous editions of *The Economics of Macro Issues* have made suggestions to improve the pedagogical usefulness of the text. Consequently, I have added the following pedagogical aids to help the student reader and the instructor:

1. *Key terms*—All key terms italicized within each chapter are defined prior to each chapter.

2. *Summary*—Every chapter includes a short one-paragraph summary indicating the salient points that the student should have retained from the chapter.

3. *Discussion questions*—Two or three discussion questions are found at the end of each chapter. These can be used for classroom discussion or homework assignments.

Acknowledgments

I have received numerous comments and criticisms from users of this book throughout the last few years. To all of you, I extend my appreciation. I also wish to especially thank the following reviewers who provided detailed comments and who helped me in revising this book. They are:

Richard Keehn, University of Wisconsin at Parkside

Paul J. Magelli, Wichita State University

James B. O'Neill, University of Delaware

All errors remain my sole responsibility. I continue to welcome comments and criticisms from adopters of this text.

RLM

Coral Gables

PART ONE

The
Government
Sector,
Taxation,
and the
Distribution
of Income

A Constitutional Amendment to Balance the Federal Budget

Key Terms

balanced budget A situation in which the federal government's tax receipts just equal its expenditures.

deficit spending Federal government spending that exceeds tax receipts. Deficit spending is financed by the sale of U.S. Treasury government securities.

GNP (Gross National Product) The market value over one year of all final goods and services produced.

transfers Payments governments make to individuals for which no concurrent goods and services are given in exchange by those individuals—e.g., food stamps and welfare payments.

Article V of the United States Constitution directs Congress to call a convention when two-thirds of the states' legislators petition it to do so. By 1982, thirty-one of the required thirty-four states had in fact called for a constitutional convention to draft a **balanced budget** amendment. Congress clearly is on the hot seat. If three more states act, Congress either has to propose an amendment or allow a constitutional convention to draft one.

In general, the federal government does not like to see the states' governments exercising their only true power over the federal government. To prevent this power from being exercised the federal government has at times threatened retaliation if certain states "signed up" for a constitutional convention. For example, when the constitutional convention movement was gathering momentum under the Carter administration, word came down from Washington that it would retaliate by cutting revenue sharing and public works expenditures in the offending states. Those states that were threatened backed down.

When Reagan was elected, a number of states put constitutional conventional issues aside, hoping the new administration would prove constitutional reform unnecessary. How? By bringing the budget under control and eliminating the deficits. By 1981, all bets were off, with a $100-billion-plus deficit in the making. The thought of a federally balanced budget became a pure pipe dream to most. Some even talked about a $300 billion deficit by 1986. History seems to concur with the budget pessimists. Over the last 51 years, there were only nine surpluses totaling $34.1 billion and forty-two deficits totaling $684.1 billion. And it didn't seem to matter whether a Democrat or a Republican was in office. Since the 1930s, Republicans have had only a slightly better record of balancing the budget than the Democrats. The Hoover, Eisenhower, Nixon, and Ford administrations had four surpluses and fifteen deficits. Democrats Roosevelt, Truman, Kennedy, Johnson, and Carter produced five surpluses and twenty-seven deficits. However, the cumulative budget deficits over each president's term expressed as a proportion of total output of goods and services shows a somewhat different story. The record is seen in Table 1-1.

So, according to some, the future looks grim unless a balanced budget amendment is passed by the Congress. But is a constitutional convention likely? According to legal experts, even if the required thirty-four states pass resolutions to have a constitutional convention, there are still many legal uncer-

TABLE 1-1 Cumulative Budget Deficits as a Proportion of Total National Output of Goods and Services

Hoover (R)	1.7%
Roosevelt (D)	14.0%
Truman (D)	.2%
Eisenhower (R)	.5%
Kennedy (D)	1.1%
Johnson (D)	.9%
Nixon (R)	1.2%
Ford (R)	3.6%
Carter (D)	2.1%

tainties. There is no precedent and nothing specific in the Constitution about what to do. Can the convention be limited to one specific issue? Does Congress have the legal authority to set the ground rules? No one really knows the answers to these and other important questions. One of the problems is that the resolutions passed by the various states and sent to Congress are not identical; they seek at least ten different forms of a constitutional amendment to balance the budget.

Does balancing the budget mean limiting spending? Of course there are literally hundreds of arguments against an amendment to balance the budget. Some people maintain that this would eliminate Congress's ability to act on pressing social problems. Others believe that such an amendment would be unworkable because it is difficult to determine what constitutes federal government spending. Still others point out that a balanced budget says nothing about limiting the growth and size of the federal government. Indeed, critics point out that even though most *states* have constitutional provisions requiring a balanced budget, such provisions have not prevented both taxes and state spending from rising more rapidly than the incomes of the citizens of those states.

Proponents of a conventional constitutional amendment are not convinced by these arguments. They argue that a balanced budget amendment would keep the federal government out of the credit markets. Also, such an amendment presumably would signal that the federal government was going to maintain spending discipline.

Perhaps the issue of a balanced budget is somewhat beside the point. To be sure, federal budget deficits have an impact on credit markets and interest rates. To be sure, the ability of Congress to run budget deficits perhaps does not limit spending enough. But, from a societal point of view, the true impact of government is not basically a function of the size of the deficit. Rather, the true impact of government, at least from one point of view, depends solely on the total size of government spending. The way in which government is financed does not ultimately determine that size. Taxation or **deficit spending** (selling U.S. Treasury bonds) can finance government. So can printing money. But in the end, the people finance government. If forty percent of the **GNP** is taken by federal, state, and local governments and then put back into the economy via government expenditures on goods and services and **transfers** to individuals, does it matter how that forty percent was obtained? Perhaps it does from a political point of view. If a constitutional amendment makes deficits illegal, then taxes would have to be raised to match government expenditures. Perhaps this explicit form of government finance would present a clearer signal to the electorate about the true size of government. Thus, a constitutional amendment to require a balanced budget might simply be put under the category of "full disclosure" or "truth in labeling." No one ever said there was anything wrong about the American public learning the facts.

Summary

A constitutional convention to pass a balanced budget amendment might occur as a response to the electorate's concern with continuing high federal government deficits. Federal government deficits have occurred in over eighty percent of the years in the last half century. They have occurred with Republicans and with Democrats. Balancing the budget does not necessarily mean limiting federal spending. Government spending is obtained either by taxation, deficit spending (i.e., selling U.S. Treasury bonds), or printing money. The way in which government is financed does not necessarily determine the size of government.

Discussion Questions

1. If it does not matter how government is financed, then why would individuals and politicians worry so much about the size of the federal budget deficit every year?

2. Would a balanced budget amendment limit Congress's ability to act on pressing social problems?

The Subterranean Economy

Key Terms

subterranean economy The underground or cash economy in which transactions are not reported.

marginal tax rate The income tax rate in percentage terms applied to the last dollars of income earned that fall into the last tax bracket.

unemployment rate The percentage of the measured labor force that is looking for a job but unable to find one.

There is an economy out there unlike the economy that everyone talks about. It is called the **subterranean economy.** That does not mean it involves transactions that take place in caves. Rather, it is the economy consisting of unreported economic exchanges. It is also called the cash economy. Of course, we have always had some part of our economy that has been subterranean or unreported. That is the illegal part—gambling, prostitution, and narcotics. Those economic activities are not fully reflected in the government's official statistics on total economic activity, for obvious reasons. The participants of the subterranean economy are not just dope pushers, gamblers, prostitutes, and the Mafia. Perhaps the most significant fraction of that underground, unreported economy consists of citizens in good standing in their communities. Let's take a look at some common examples.

West Virginia coal miners picking ginseng roots in the summer often do not report the extra $1,000 or so that they earn. Physicians in Los Angeles and elsewhere routinely pressure their patients into paying cash and just as routinely underreport their income by about one-third. Carpenters in New Jersey take part of their pay "off the books" and part on; some are "entirely off the books." Musicians in New Orleans work "some gigs on the books, some gigs off the books." In New York City, the temptation to "skip the sales tax" and engage in cash transactions is great because it means not paying the local eight-percent sales tax.

The preceding examples can be multiplied by at least a million, and still all the ways in which the subterranean economy works would not be fully explained. Why do individuals want to engage in cash transactions? In most situations, the answer is simple: To avoid taxes. All those individuals—from the carpenter to the ginseng-root picker to the general physician—who don't report income are thereby avoiding federal withholding tax, perhaps state income tax, and Social Security taxes. The greater the individual **marginal tax rate,** the greater the incentive to join the fast-growing subterranean economy.

Another good reason to avoid being "on the books" is to be able to continue receiving unemployment benefits or other welfare payments. Musicians, for example, often will work "on the books" for awhile in order to be eligible for unemployment insurance. When they go on unemployment insurance, they will play "off the books" until the unemployment money runs out. Then they'll do another job "on the books" to qualify again. This phenomenon, of course, is not peculiar to musicians. Waitresses, day laborers, and thousands of other workers engage in it.

Avoiding sales taxes is another incentive to join the underground economy. In New York City, for example, a number of retailers will sell a camera to a New York City resident but "suggest" that an empty box be mailed to an out-of-state address. That way the retailer doesn't have to pay sales taxes because the camera presumably is shipped out of state, and, of course, the purchaser doesn't pay sales taxes either. By law, out-of-state merchants must collect and remit New York sales taxes if they deliver within the state. Nonetheless, a large number of New Jersey stores are more than willing to deliver expensive appliances, rugs, and furniture to New York City residents tax free and often without delivery charges. All one needs to do is open the Manhattan Yellow Pages, which constitutes a tax-free shoppers' bible. They list dealers in TVs and cameras from virtually every contiguous state. How much does the city of New York lose in sales taxes through the underground economy and various other illegal devices? Some believe the losses are as much as $250 million a year.

"Skimming" is another word for engaging in nonreported income-producing activities. Typical businesses that engage in moderate to heavy amounts of skimming are retail outlets, taverns and bars, flea-market-type selling companies, and so on. A few years ago, a skimming scandal involved taverns on Chicago's north side. The *Chicago Sun-Times* and the city's Better Government Association bought a tavern, which they planned to use to get first-hand evidence of corruption among city inspectors. Instead, they opened the whole can of worms called skimming. The first time the new owners went to a business broker, he said, "First, we should talk about tax fraud. You can't judge a tavern until you know how much it takes off the top." Some of the posted listings openly referred to skimming—for example, "Gross business—$41,800 with 20 percent adjustment. In reality, around $60,000."

The subterranean economy has led to what is known in the banking industry as "the big bill phenomenon." From 1967 to

1978, the value of $100 bills in circulation rose by more than 250 percent to $32.9 billion. When you compare this to the total value of currency in circulation, which rose by only 125 percent, you know something has happened. Additional evidence about the increased use of $100 bills is that the ratio of $100 bills to GNP final sales increased sharply. Had the 1967 ratio held, we would have about $10 billion less in $100 bills outstanding. Of course, some of this excess is due to inflation, but one would expect it to be minimal given the sizable increase in credit card business.

What does all this underground economy activity mean? It may mean that the nation is experiencing more economic growth and less unemployment than we've been told. GNP may be rising at a much greater rate than government statistics indicate. One estimate in 1981 was that the subterranean economy accounted for a mindboggling $300 billion, or over 10 percent of the recorded gross national product. Further, to the extent that the subterranean economy grows faster than the legal economy, the rate of economic growth is being understated by GNP numbers. Additionally, official **unemployment rates** may be overstating actual unemployment. Furthermore, the number of families actually living below the poverty line may be less than the official estimate. We can predict that, as long as marginal tax rates remain high or increase, the incentive to join the underground economy will remain the same or increase. Thus, we will have less confidence that government GNP statistics are really telling us how fast our economy is growing.

Summary

The underground, or subterranean, economy exists for two reasons: (1) because certain activities are illegal and therefore individuals do not want to have records of those activities having taken place, and (2) because high marginal tax rates give people an incentive to obtain income without reporting it. A relatively small portion of today's subterranean economy is concerned with illegal activities. The rest is comprised of individuals attempting to reduce their taxable income in a variety of ways, such as working "off the books," not recording sales in order to avoid sales taxes, engaging in business "skimming," and so on. The underground economy will continue to exist as long as marginal tax rates continue to exist. It may account for well over ten percent of recorded gross national product.

Discussion Questions

1. Give at least two reasons why shopping by mail has become so popular in recent years in the United States.

2. To what extent do marginal tax rates determine the growth of the subterranean economy?

Other Ways of Avoiding Taxes

Key Terms

barter The exchange of goods for goods and services, or services for goods and services, without the use of money.

tax bracket A specified interval of income to which a specific and unique marginal tax rate is applied.

opportunity cost The cost of doing something measured in terms of the loss of the opportunity to pursue the next best alternative activity with the same resources.

consumer durables Goods that have a useful life of more than a year, such as houses and automobiles.

substitution effect The effect on quantity demanded due to a change in relative price only; quantity demanded rises when the relative price falls.

income effect The effect on quantity demanded resulting from an implicit change in income due to a change in the price of a commodity purchased.

The subterranean economy involves doing things "off the books." Related to such activities are other methods of avoiding taxes. They include out-and-out barter, do-it-yourself activities, the purchase of durable goods, and leisure.

Barter existed in America even before Peter Minuit got the Indians to trade some blankets and beads for Manhattan Island in 1626. However, barter is a costly way of making exchanges, for it requires a double coincidence of wants. In other words, a person selling a particular product, such as shoes, who wants another product, such as tomatoes, must find someone who at the same time has tomatoes and wants shoes. That is where the double coincidence comes in, and the probability of that occurring, of course, is very small. It is much more rational to use money as a medium of exchange. Nonetheless, barter has been coming back in recent years, and not for the reasons you might think. It has little to do with the higher cost of living or inflation in general. Rather, it's considered yet another way to avoid paying income taxes.

Take a simple example. A dentist needs approximately $1,000 worth of legal services to set up a new pension plan, while a lawyer coincidentally needs approximately $1,000 worth of gold inlays to replace silver fillings. Assume that both are in the fifty-percent **tax bracket;** thus, if they individually purchased the needed services, each would have to earn $2,000 in order to have $1,000 after taxes to pay for those services. If, on the other hand, they make a trade by bartering legal services for dental care, no taxes will be paid if the deal is kept from the IRS. They each will be saving $1,000 in taxes but will end up with exactly the same amount of services they wished to buy in the first place. (Remember, the dentist's service to the lawyer and the lawyer's service to the dentist are both forms of income worth a total of $2,000.)

The IRS is aware of the new barter society and looks at it with a wary eye. Of course, barter arrangements are difficult for the IRS to track down when people don't declare them. The law on this matter is clear, however: You are supposed to declare income realized in any form.

There is a growing number of barter groups throughout the nation. The Useful Services Exchange is a nonprofit clearing-house in Reston, Virginia. The Learning Exchange in Evanston, Illinois, probably has 50,000 participants by now. The Vacation

Exchange Club allows people to barter houses for their vacation time, as does the Holiday Home Bureau. The Business Owners' Exchange in Minneapolis has about 500 members, including lawyers, dentists, and CPAs. Each member of the Exchange must pay a $150 fee; then members can trade their professional services, as well as cars, boats, and so on. The Exchange issues checks that look like commercial bank checks and sends members monthly statements listing sales and purchases, although no real money is exchanged. The United Trade Club in San Jose, California, has almost 2,000 members, also including doctors and lawyers. Indeed, bartering is back.

Rather than earning income that is taxable to hire someone to repair or maintain your home, you can provide the services yourself, not declare those do-it-yourself activities as income, and avoid paying taxes. The do-it-yourself society has increased dramatically in the United States, in part because of rising repair and construction costs, but also because individuals in higher tax brackets find it beneficial to avoid taxes this way.

People generally agree that do-it-yourself operations are considerably less expensive than work done by professionals. But now let's consider an example that shows how doing it yourself also means escaping taxes on the added value of your own work.

Mr. Jones, who is in the fifty-percent tax bracket, wants to panel his den. The cost will be $400 for materials if he does the work himself versus an extra $600 for the labor if he hires a professional. That comes to $1,000, and he must earn $2,000 before taxes in order to have that $1,000. To buy only the materials, he would need to earn $800 to have the $400 if he does the work himself. Another way of looking at the situation is that Mr. Jones can generate the equivalent of $600 in labor value if he does the work himself. Because Uncle Sam does not tax that $600, taxes are legally avoided. Of course, the decision to engage in do-it-yourself activities is also a function of **opportunity costs.** If Mr. Jones's opportunity cost is *very* high, he may not necessarily opt for the do-it-yourself choice. Taxes are, to be sure, legally avoided by doing it yourself, but opportunity cost is never avoided. If Mr. Jones uses up $5,000 in opportunity cost—income that he could have received had he not been doing it himself—then the taxes saved by doing it himself are trivial in comparison.

It seems that even when we have a downturn in business activity in this country, the sales of Mercedes, Rolls Royces, and other luxury cars just keep rising. Even when there is a downturn in Britain, new Rolls Royces keep showing up on the street. What is the explanation for this shift toward more luxurious cars? Is it because tastes have changed, or is it because so many of us are so much richer? These are possible explanations, but a more important determinant exists. It has to do with the nature of progressive personal income taxes and the attempt by individuals to avoid paying relatively high tax rates.

Let's ignore for the moment the depreciation, insurance, gas, and other operating costs of a Rolls Royce or a Mercedes. Consider only the opportunity cost of the money tied up in such an expensive car. Remember that opportunity cost is the value of the next highest alternative use. Consider a person with $100,000 who lives in London. The choice is between a new Rolls Royce and income-earning investments such as stocks, bonds, or real estate. Assume that the $100,000 could earn ten percent interest, or $10,000. This is the before-tax rate of return. In England, it is possible to be taxed at a marginal tax rate on investment income as high as ninety-eight percent! Assume that this very rich person is in the ninety-eight-percent tax bracket. The after-tax return on the invested $100,000 will only be $.02 × $10,000 = $200. What, then, is the true annual opportunity cost of plunking down $100,000 for a Rolls Royce rather than putting it into a ten-percent income-yielding asset? Only $200.

In the United States marginal tax rates do not go that high, but for many people they are fifty percent. A new Mercedes that ties up, say, $40,000 in wealth here could have yielded, say, $4,000 in before-tax returns. But if a person is in the fifty-percent tax bracket, the after-tax yield drops to .5 × $4,000 = $2,000.

Clearly, if your marginal tax bracket is only fourteen percent, your opportunity cost of tying up a large amount of money in a luxury car will be approximately equal to what you could earn in the highest-yielding alternative investment. Therefore, we can state that the higher your marginal tax bracket, the "cheaper" will be the purchase of a Mercedes or a Rolls Royce, other things being equal. Thus, higher income not only induces individuals to buy more expensive cars just because those in-dividuals are richer but also because, by being in a higher marginal tax bracket, the opportunity cost of consuming so extravagantly falls.

We've talked about only Rolls Royces and Mercedes, but this same analysis can be applied to all **consumer durables**— that is, purchased items that last for more than a year or so. Stereos, houses, yachts, tennis courts, and hot tubs all share the same feature: They are alternative investment options that an individual has. The greater one's marginal tax bracket, the lower the opportunity cost of owning such consumer durables. The general shift toward more expensive cars, bigger yachts, and more luxurious houses may now make more sense.

Finally, one of the best ways to avoid taxes is simply not to work. After all, leisure is still an untaxed activity. What is the income from leisure? The joy and pleasure you receive from it. How much do you pay for leisure? Your potential *after-tax* income. Notice the emphasis on after-tax, for that is the true cost of not working. If you are making ten dollars an hour but your marginal tax rate is fifty percent, you are only giving up five dollars if you work one hour less. It's not surprising that individuals may wish to buy more leisure the higher their mar-ginal tax rate, for the relative price of leisure falls because of that high marginal tax rate. Of course, there is an offsetting effect: You have less income to spend as the marginal tax rate rises. But whenever the **substitution effect**, due to the lower relative price of leisure, outweighs the **income effect**, you will work less.

Deciding to take an increasing proportion of your income in the form of leisure may be the most pleasant way of all to avoid paying more income taxes.

Summary

Even though barter is an inefficient means of economic exchange, individuals use it increasingly, to avoid having to report income and pay income taxes. Engaging in do-it-yourself activities also reduces tax burdens because taxable income is not earned to pay for the work done—the work is done by the individual outside of the marketplace. High marginal tax rates also encourage the purchase of consumer durables rather than normal income-earning investments, such as stocks or bonds. After all, the income earned on those investments is taxable, so individuals in high marginal tax brackets face a lower opportunity cost if they decide to purchase consumer durables instead. Finally, one way to avoid taxes is not to work—to buy more leisure.

Discussion Questions

1. In 1981 the highest marginal tax rate in the U.S. dropped from seventy percent to fifty percent. Does the analysis presented in this chapter still hold?

2. Has the growth in garage sales and yard sales had anything to do with avoiding taxes?

The
18% Solution—
Loopholes Beware

Key Terms

tax loopholes Legal methods of reducing taxes owed to governments.

tax-exempt municipal bonds Bonds offered by municipal government, the yearly earned interest of which is exempt from federal, and sometimes state and local, income taxes.

tax write-offs Legitimate expenses from investments that are deducted from taxable income to reduce taxes owed.

tax shelters The array of investment outlets that allow for reducing tax liabilities legally through large tax write-offs.

median income The income level above which fifty percent of all income earners fall and below which fifty percent of all income earners fall.

bracket creep or taxflation The process by which inflation pushes individuals and corporations into higher and higher marginal tax brackets simply because of inflation.

proportional, or flat-rate, tax system A system in which all income is taxed at exactly the same rate no matter what the level of income.

degressive tax system A tax system in which the first dollars earned, such as $10,000, are not taxed at all and all income after those first dollars is taxed at a flat rate.

Tax loopholes—perfectly legal ways to avoid taxes—riddle our federal tax system. They occur in many forms, such as **tax-exempt municipal bonds,** special **tax write-offs** from investing in oil and gas, and myriad other so-called **tax shelters.** The U.S. Treasury has estimated its loss of tax revenues due to such loopholes as high as $80 billion dollars in 1983. To understand why loopholes have come into existence, one must first look at the history of our tax system and then look at the current tax incentive structure facing Americans.

Congress passed the first income tax law in 1913. That law provided for a one-percent tax on incomes over $3,000 for single individuals and $4,000 for married couples. That seems like a low income today, but back then only three percent of American wage earners had incomes exceeding those cutoff points. On income over $20,000 a tax of up to seven percent was levied. This tax went up during World War I but came down again following the war. Tax rates doubled from 1939 to 1941 and doubled again between 1941 and 1947. Even so, in 1947 the effective tax rate was only 8.4 percent. Eighty percent of families in the United States had annual incomes of less than $5,000. A person making $5,000 paid around $420 in income taxes plus $30 in Social Security taxes. On the last dollar earned, that person was paying a marginal tax rate of less than twenty percent.

The times have changed. From 1965 to 1983, marginal tax rates rose from seventeen percent to twenty-five percent for a family of four earning the **median income.** For anybody lucky enough to be earning twice the median income, marginal tax rates increased during that same time period from twenty-two percent to forty-three percent. Social Security taxes have also risen dramatically from that mere $30 in 1947 to $2,170 in 1982, or a change of 7,233 percent.

Now we come to the tax system and incentives facing Americans. Back in 1913 loopholes were certainly not a big deal. Why should they have been? Only three percent of American wage earners were paying any income tax at all. There was little financial incentive to find legal avoidance schemes for reducing one's tax liabilities. That is no longer the case, however. As the average family has found itself being pushed into higher and higher tax brackets because of inflation and rising real income, more and more Americans have found it worthwhile to seek legal tax avoidance schemes. **Bracket creep, or taxflation,** has indeed created a whole new class of potential beneficiaries from tax loophole schemes. Consider the family earning twice the median income. In 1965 its marginal tax rate was twenty-two percent. That meant that for every dollar it could keep from being taxed, that family kept twenty-two more cents in its pocket. In 1982, however, the family earning double the median income faced a forty-four-percent marginal tax bracket. That meant that it was twice as beneficial to find a way to avoid paying taxes on those last dollars of income. After all, one dollar that was somehow not taxable meant an additional forty-four cents in that family's pocket. Of course, the situation—incentive structure—for those individuals who, during World War II, were making large incomes and were therefore faced with a ninety-four-percent marginal tax rate was even more blatant. And those individuals with large incomes up until 1982 faced a maximum marginal tax rate of seventy percent— every dollar of income that became nontaxable meant seventy cents in pocket. The entire tax shelter industry was created as a result of high marginal tax rates. Why? Because of the incentive to find ways to avoid taxes the high marginal tax rates breed.

In chapter 2 we also found out that the existence and growth of the subterranean economy is a direct result of rising marginal tax rates in the United States.

Enter the eighteen-percent solution. The way to eliminate the entire tax loophole problem is to eliminate the incentive. How? By altering our current federal progressive tax system to one that assesses an eighteen-percent **proportional, or flat**

rate, tax on all income above a certain cutoff point. This solution has been offered by not only conservative economists and politicians, but by liberal Democratic senators and members of Congress. Six bills were introduced in Congress in 1982 that in one way or another called for immediate adoption of the flat tax or for studies of its feasibility. The idea behind a flat tax is that all income is taxed once, and all types of income are taxed at the same rate. Few or no deductions would be allowed. Very poor households would pay no tax at all. Actually, this flat tax proposal is more properly called a **degressive tax system.** Such a degressive tax system might not tax all income under, say, $10,000 and would tax income above $10,000 at eighteen percent.

But what would happend to federal tax revenues? According to most studies, a flat tax of eighteen percent (or somewhere in that range) would produce about the same revenues as our current tax system. Three things would occur to bring about the tax revenue equality between an eighteen-percent flat tax system and the current graduated system that goes up to fifty percent: (1) Much of the underground economy would come into the open because it would not pay to hide income illegally; (2) The tax shelter business would go out of business, again because it would not pay to engage in it; (3) There would be more investment, saving, and real work and less time spent on tax avoidance.

Summary

Our federal personal income tax system is riddled with loopholes and is extremely complicated. The reason for this is that marginal tax rates have increased for most Americans and businesses so that now it pays many Americans to seek legal ways to avoid taxes. Proposals calling for a tax reform in which the first, say, $10,000 of income is not taxed at all but the rest is taxed at a flat eighteen percent would eliminate much of the incentive to seek tax loopholes. The elimination of numerous business and medical deductions (and others) from the tax system would lead to a less complicated tax return for both households and businesses. Presumably an eighteen-percent flat tax would yield the same revenues as are currently yielded by our present tax system because less time and effort would be allocated to tax avoidance and tax evasion.

Discussion Questions

1. If the eighteen-percent flat tax were instituted for our current system, what would happen to the demand for tax accountants and tax lawyers?

2. How would a flat tax system affect the incentive of upper-income individuals and corporations to spend resources lobbying in Congress for changes in the tax laws (i.e., for tax loopholes)?

Are We Winning the War Against Poverty?

Key Terms

in-kind transfers Transfers of actual goods and services rather than money income for which no concurrent exchange of goods or services is provided—e.g., medical care or public housing.

implicit rental income The value of the services received from owning a house but not actually having to pay for those services. Such income can be estimated by what it would cost to rent the same type of house or apartment.

The bottom twenty percent of income earners are still earning about five percent of total money income in the United States, even though we have a progressive income tax and have waged a number of "wars on poverty." Data from the Bureau of the Census show the following:

TABLE 5-1

Families	Percentage of Money Income Share 1947	1981
Top 20%	43.1	41.0
Fourth 20%	23.1	22.8
Third 20%	17.0	18.1
Second 20%	11.8	12.4
Bottom 20%	5.0	5.7

Source: U.S. Bureau of Census

The same Bureau of Census data have shown that as of 1980, 29.3 million Americans still live below the federal poverty line. That seems to be a rather small drop from the 33 million who lived in poverty before Lyndon Johnson's Great Society started to pump billions of dollars into alleviating the poverty problem.

Poverty, of course, is officially defined in a culturally relative manner. A statistician at the Social Security Administration devised the poverty index by using a nutritionally adequate economy food budget for various family sizes. This budget was the result of an Agricultural Department household consumption survey done in 1955 and 1961. Thus, in 1965 the poverty line was $3,165 annual income for a family of four. In 1980, after adjustments for inflation, it was set at $8,414 annual income for a family of four. Critics of the poverty index believe that it is deficient because it is still based on the 1955 and 1961 studies, which do not take account of the needs of the poor today.

Whatever the line should be—either higher or lower than it is—the real gut issue concerns continued inequality of income in the United States. Poverty is merely the most apparent manifestation of whatever inequality continues to exist. Using the data presented in Table 5-1 and comparing it with similar data collected in other countries, we find that the degree of inequality that exists in America is 100 percent more than that in Sweden, 50 percent more than that in Japan, and 36 percent more than that in West Germany. If accurate, these comparisons are striking. But are they accurate? A number of researchers in the United States have begun to doubt the validity of the Census Bureau figures in this country and, by implication, of similarly obtained figures in other countries.

The first serious questioning of Census Bureau income distribution data seems to have been done by a Virginia economist, Edgar G. Browning. In several published studies, he came to the conclusion that there is less income inequality in the United States than meets the Census Bureau's eye. Specifically, he contends that the share of total income going to the bottom twenty percent of income earners has more than doubled since World War II! Table 5-2 shows the distribution of total income according to Browning's computations. Not only does it show that the bottom twenty percent of income earners have increased their share, but it also shows that the top twenty percent have suffered a reduction. In other words, if Browning is correct, income inequality is lessening in the United States.

How could such a change have taken place without the Census Bureau picking it up? It all has to do with the definition of income. The Census Bureau figures—those cited at the beginning of this chapter—relate to *money* income only, rather than total income. The reason that this narrow definition may be inadequate today is because numerous relatively poorer individuals receive what are called **in-kind transfers** from the government. These are in the form of Medicaid, Medicare, food stamps, housing subsidies, school lunches, and so on, which were relatively unimportant until about 1966. For example, in 1965, they constituted only $2.3 billion of government expenditures; in 1976, that number had grown to $50 billion. If an individual household receives, say, $2,500 of in-kind transfers such as school lunches and housing subsidies, these transfers will not be included in the Census Bureau's definition of money income. Thus, that family will be classified as being poorer than it actually is. It is the inclusion of in-kind benefits received by the bottom twenty percent of income earners that changes the income distribution statistics so radically.

TABLE 5-2

Families	Percentage of Total Income Share
Top 20%	31.9
Fourth 20%	20.9
Third 20%	18.4
Second 20%	16.1
Bottom 20%	12.6

Source: Edgar Browning, "The Trend Toward Equality in the Distribution of Net Income," *Southern Economic Journal*, July 1976, Table IV.

Another thing we must realize about the bottom twenty percent of income earners is that many of them are retirees. They may be earning little *current* income, but their actual spendable income would pull them out of the bottom twenty-percent bracket. The reason they have more actual spendable income than current *measured* income is because many of them are able to draw down their substantial wealth. After all, there is a life cycle of wealth accumulation. Young individuals may have little or no wealth; but, as they accumulate more savings, they enter into higher wealth brackets, and eventually they start "dissaving"—that is, drawing on their wealth—particularly when they reach retirement age. And as persons approach the end of their expected lifetime, their wealth generally decreases dramatically. Therefore, there is a period after retirement when retirees use up their accumulated savings. The case in point would be a retired couple who had been paying on a house for twenty-five years. At the time they retire, let us say, their house payments are finished. They continue to live in the house and reap the **implicit rental income** during their retired years, but this implicit rental income does not show up in official money income statistics.

A few years after Browning's research was completed, a separate study by the Congressional Budget Office (CBO) reached the same conclusion. It concluded that the number of poor in 1977 was not 26 million but 9 million. The Census Bureau figures show that fifteen percent of Americans over sixty-five are living in poverty; the CBO study shows that only four percent are living in poverty. The director of the CBO, Alice M. Rivlin, contends that "the nation has come a lot closer to eliminating poverty than most people realize."

Not everyone agrees with Browning or Rivlin, however. Soon after the CBO study was published, Michael Harrington, author of *The Other America* and possible originator of the first "war on poverty," stated that "the poor are being made invisible again." [1] Harrington believes that "the [statistical] procedure is to take all of the factors—some real, some imagined—that might conceivably have led to an overcounting of the poor and to give them the greatest weight possible." [2] Harrington maintains that the official poverty index undercounts the poor by a large number. He also notes that the CBO values the in-kind transfer benefits received by the poor at their dollar cost to the federal government. The assumption made here, of course, is that the in-kind transfer income received from the government is equivalent to cash income. Is it accurate to state that such valuations of in-kind transfer income overstate the true utility obtained by the recipients? Had the recipients received cash instead of in-kind transfers, they undoubtedly would have purchased a different market basket of goods, which would have yielded a higher level of satisfaction. Thus, to the extent that they receive less satisfaction than they would have received from cash, Harrington's criticism must be accepted.

Other critics of the studies by Browning and the Congressional Budget Office question, in particular, the assumption that Medicare and Medicaid benefits are income. These critics contend that if such analyses were carried to their logical conclusion, it would mean that the sicker the poor are, the less poor they become because they would be receiving more Medicare

---

[1] Michael Harrington, "Hiding the Other America," *New Republic* (February 26, 1977), pp. 15–17.

[2] Ibid., p. 16.

and Medicaid. These in-kind transfers would be added to the total income for statistical purposes.

And so the debate rages on. Alice Rivlin is sticking by her office's study. The Department of Health and Human Services is revising its poverty index on the basis of a 1965 food survey combined with the more recent Agricultural Department "thrifty food budget," but it is not going to include the value of noncash benefits. Some estimate that, when the new index is revealed, the number of officially defined poor will increase by twenty-five percent. Thus, the question will remain: Are there really more or less poor people in the United States than there were a quarter of a century ago?

Summary

The distribution of money income as measured by the Bureau of the Census has not changed very much since the end of World War II. If one includes in-kind transfers in total income, however, the data show that the bottom twenty percent of wage earners have increased their share of total income since World War II. One must be careful about valuing in-kind transfers at their cost to the government, because if individuals were given cash instead of in-kind transfers, they would undoubtedly spend it in a different way. Also, Medicare and Medicaid expenditures can hardly be counted dollar-for-dollar as an increase in income. Nonetheless, statistics on poverty do not count the implicit income that many individuals, especially older people, have from their accumulated wealth, particularly in the form of paid-for housing.

Discussion Questions

1. What does it mean to say that the definition of poverty is relative, not absolute?

2. Why do you think government statisticians have normally refused to include the value of in-kind transfers as part of poor people's total income?

PART TWO

Business
Cycles

Problemſ in
Meaſuring GNP

Key Terms

intermediate goods Goods that contribute to present or future consumer welfare but are not a direct source of satisfaction in themselves—e.g., transportation expenses to work and other business expenses.

consumption The using up of goods and services that have an exchangeable value.

Overall business activity in any country never seems to stay the same. There are ups ("booms") and there are downs ("busts" and recessions), even though the long-term trend may be up. Even noneconomists can agree on some of the obvious signs of an "up" in business activity—expanding corporate profits, higher employment, increased business investment spending— and the obvious signs of "down" periods—rising unemployment, falling profits, increased idle production capacity. But it appears that the one overall *measure* of business activity is no longer considered appropriate. This overall measure is gross national product, or GNP, which is a measure of the total market value of final goods and services produced in any one year in the United States.

The way GNP is measured has been under attack for some time. What is the meaning of an increase in GNP due to an increase in the production and sale of pollution control equipment that is required because other producers are fouling the air and polluting the water, the costs of which were ignored? That is just one complaint that critics of GNP measurement lodge. There are many other complaints, but there are also ways to accommodate them, at least on a theoretical level.

To "correct" GNP, we need to add what is not measured but what nonetheless involves production, and we need to subtract what is included but involves no basic increase in economic satisfaction. Some additions are already made to GNP that are not actually worked through the market economy. The implicit rental value of owner-occupied housing is added, as well as an estimate of the food produced and consumed on the farm. Do-it-yourself activities (encouraged by high marginal tax rates) are not. However, they constitute the production of a service. If you take your car to a mechanic, the services performed on the car end up as part of GNP. But if you and a friend repair your car, these services are not included in GNP.

The biggest category of do-it-yourself services left out of GNP are those performed in the house by homemakers. The value of the services performed by homemakers who are not explicitly paid can indeed be large. Every year the Chase Manhattan Bank of New York estimates the value of homemakers' services based on the going wage rates that would have to be paid to provide those services if the homemaker did not. By now, the *weekly* value of a homemaker's services is estimated to be over $400. However, homemakers' services not counted in GNP are declining, as more and more services in the home are purchased in the marketplace. Each time the homemaker has another individual or firm do something, that part of home services will be counted in GNP.

In some "true" measure of GNP, we should probably add the value of illegal activities like gambling, prostitution, and bootlegging, because such activities often generate satisfaction to the individuals engaging in them. Also to be included is income that is illegally not reported by income tax evaders.

Lastly, our increased leisure (relative to income) must be included in a corrected measure of GNP. After all, leisure is a good, and it is scarce. It has value and generates satisfaction. For the civilian economy, average weekly hours worked have fallen from over forty-eight in 1943 to around thirty-six in 1982, a definite increase in the real standard of living of those enjoying more leisure time.

What about those things that should be subtracted from GNP, such as expenditures sometimes referred to as "regrettable necessities"? These regrettables include expenditures for prestige, diplomacy, national security, space research and technology, and police, fire, and prison expenditures. Also to be subtracted from GNP are what are called **intermediate goods**— that is, goods that contribute to present or future consumer welfare but are not yet direct sources of utility themselves. Included in intermediate goods would be personal business expenses, transporation expenses, and so on. Disamenities of urbanization are generally considered as costs to be subtracted from GNP and include congestion, noise, litter, and pollution.

Two economists have come up with a measure of what they call MEW, or measure of economic welfare. William Nordhaus and James Tobin use various techniques to try to estimate disamenities of urbanization, regrettable necessities, intermediate goods, and so on. When they adjust GNP, they come up with an estimated MEW. Perhaps this is a step in the right direction. Nordhaus's and Tobin's estimates indicate that the true consumption possibilities of the nation have been growing, just as GNP has, but at a slower rate. Critics of MEW, however, point out that the estimates used to adjust GNP are extremely crude and rely on the authors' own value judgments concerning the classification of goods into consumption or intermediate ones. Furthermore, even if MEW were an accurate measure, it measures only consumption and not economic welfare. Welfare can be derived from the amount of utility, happiness, or satisfaction received from **consumption**. MEW assumes that welfare is proportional to consumption, which may indeed not be the case.

Summary

The official measurement of gross national product may not give an accurate representation of economic well-being. To improve official GNP statistics we should add the value of do-it-yourself activities and, in particular, the value of homemaker services. We probably should also add the value of some illegal activities and the value of the increased leisure we are now consuming relative to what we consumed in the past. We might want to subtract our regrettable necessities, such as expenditures on national security, and expenditures on intermediate goods, such as business transportation expenses. An important category of disamenities such as pollution, noise, and litter should be subtracted also. Unfortunately, even when we correct GNP for what is left out and what should be taken out, we do not necessarily end up with a measure of welfare or happiness.

Discussion Questions

1. How does one determine what is a final good or service and what is a regrettable necessity or an intermediate good? In other words, where does one draw the line?

2. Why can't we conclude that welfare is proportional to annual national consumption?

Is the U.S. Losing the GNP Race?

Key Terms

utility Want—satisfying power, or satisfaction in general.
foreign exchange rate The rate at which one currency can be exchanged for another currency.

"U.S. Slips to Fourth Place in the GNP Race." "U.S. Gets Beaten Again by Switzerland, Sweden, and Denmark."

These are the kinds of headlines that Americans are accustomed to seeing these days, for the common view is that America is losing in the per capita GNP race. Published figures from the U.S. Department of State, the International Monetary Fund, the United Nations, and other world organizations typically show that per capita GNP for the United States is $1,000 or $2,000 less than for Switzerland and Sweden and a couple of hundred dollars less than for Denmark. We have already mentioned the difficulties in correctly measuring GNP in chapter 6, and the potential downward bias due to the large subterranean economy in chapter 2. Putting those problems aside, we still end up with severe measurement problems when trying to compare per capita income in the United States to per capita income in other countries.

It is extremely difficult to compare living standards across countries because of the difficulties in standardizing the way income is measured throughout the world. We even have difficulty estimating living standards in various regions within the United States because prices are different for different items in those different regions. For example, a price index for Honolulu may be twenty percent higher than the price index for, say, Seattle. Does that mean that if you move to Honolulu with the same income you had in Seattle, you would be twenty percent poorer? Probably not, because you would *substitute* the cheaper items for the more expensive items in Honolulu. For example, you would tend to eat less fresh meat in Honolulu and substitute more frozen imported meat from New Zealand. You could tend to substitute more frequent picnics on the beach in the sun for more expensive restaurant meals. The same situation holds true when one goes from country to country. Individuals will react to changing relative prices by substituting more of the relatively cheaper commodities.

There is something else that official per capita income statistics seem to miss entirely. Income, properly measured, is not just money income but includes a host of other things that yield **utility,** or satisfaction, to individuals. As an example, consider a household that owns several cars, a boat, a stereo system, a house with a swimming pool, a sewing machine, and a few other consumer durables. For the most part, the implied income stream of utility, or satisfaction, received by this household is not counted in official government statistics on per capita income in this country or in any other. Since U.S. citizens have a dramatically higher per capita level of consumer durables, the official statistics underestimate the true relative position of Americans on the per capita income ladder.

A number of researchers have attempted to get an accurate handle on the true relative standard of living positions of the United States and other countries. Irving B. Kravis, Alan W. Heston, and Robert Somers of the University of Pennsylvania have been involved in a United Nations statistical project for some years. The project was started because of the difficulty of comparing per capita income at any point in time due to changing exchange rates. Most international comparisons of per capita income use prevailing **foreign exchange rates** against the U.S. dollar, which is used as a common denominator. That is to say, the GNP of a foreign country, expressed in its own currency, is simply converted into dollars at the current foreign exchange rate and then divided by its population to get per capita income. Exchange rates, however, can fluctuate widely within a few months or years even though there has been no change in real output in some countries. The resulting comparison of per capita income figures, therefore, is prone to error.

The Kravis *et al* U.N. International Comparison Project focuses on purchasing power. The researchers examined actual price and spending data in different countries. In each country, an estimate of how much of each nation's currency is necessary to buy a comparable item in other countries is given. Shoes, bread, eggs, haircuts, tractors, and office buildings are some of the many commodities examined. These expenditures are typically *not* involved in international trade. Thus, exchange rates tell us nothing about their true comparative cost. Looking at what it actually takes to buy these noninternationally traded items, the researchers concluded that per capita income in Sweden and Germany is about eighty-six and seventy-six percent, respectively, of the U.S. figure. The conclusion is that "the U.S. affluence is still greater than Sweden's and Switzerland's and about twenty-five to thirty percent higher than Germany's and Denmark's on a per capita basis."

Whether we can continue to stay on top is quite another issue, though.

Summary

Individuals respond to change in relative prices. Therefore, individuals in different countries where relative prices are different will consume a different basket of goods; they substitute toward the more relatively cheaper products and away from the relatively more expensive products. So, comparative international per capita incomes may not fully indicate the relative levels of satisfaction different countries' citizens enjoy. Additionally, Americans enjoy an implicit stream of satisfaction from their relatively large stock of consumer durables. This stream of implicit income is not counted in GNP statistics. Another problem with comparing international per capita incomes is that they are all expressed in dollars using a current foreign exchange rate that may change from month to month.

Discussion Questions

1. Why do we predict that individuals will not purchase the same relative quantities of all commodities even if their incomes are the same when relative prices are different?

2. What does it mean to say that total income includes implicit income from durable goods? How would you measure that implicit income per year for an average family?

When Has a Recession Started?

Key Terms

recession A period of overall business activity when the economy is not expanding (or is even declining) as fast as it normally does.

equilibrium A situation from which there is no tendency to move and to which there is a tendency to return if there is movement away from it.

real GNP Gross national product corrected for changes in the price level.

new business capital formation Investment in additions to our capital stocks, such as new buildings and equipment.

capacity utilization The degree to which the available stock of business capital is being used in actual production.

There are many phases to the business cycle. Starting at the bottom or trough, there is a recovery phase, a boom phase, a recession phase, and, in some business cycles, an even deeper depression phase. Most people have some notion of what a boom period is, and most people have some notion of what a depression is. But at what point in the business cycle does the economy definitely move into **recession?** And at what point in the business cycle does the economy definitely pull out of a recession? As we will see, there is no one, easy answer to such questions.

If you ask a person whether he or she is sick, the answer will depend on the norm or equilibrium physical condition to which that individual is accustomed. For example, a person who has a chronic slight backache will not declare that he or she is sick on the day that the backache is felt; however, a person who has never had a backache will. Some individuals run a normal temperature above 98.6 degrees. If we declare 98.6 degrees to be normal, we would have to say that those people who permanently have a higher temperature than 98.6 are not normal; in other words, they are sick. But they may not agree. Thus, the definition of sickness depends on the normal **equilibrium** of each individual's physical state. So, too, for the economy.

An economy may not necessarily be considered "sick" just because there is no increase, on average, in the real standard of living of each member of the population. Indeed, such was the state of the world for most periods until two centuries ago. Consider, on the other hand, an economy accustomed to growth, like our own. For well over a century, we have experienced, on average, a 1.5 percent increase in our real standard of living, or in **real GNP.** In that setting, a period in which the real standard of living does not rise is a period in which the economy is "sick." And, indeed, in our own system such a period is often defined as a recession.

Most government officials accept a definition of recession that focuses on the behavior of real GNP—defined here as GNP corrected for price-level changes. Sometimes a recession is defined as any period during which real GNP does not grow for at least two quarters in a row. Now, of course, that is an arbitrary definition. Why is the criterion two quarters and not one or three of four? Only an ad hoc answer is possible. Economic theory can give no firm definition of a recession, so any definition becomes, in a sense, arbitrary.

The rate of unemployment also has a lot to do with whether or not economists believe we are in a recession; but, again, the customary norm has to be considered. Many other aspects of the economy must be taken into account when one attempts to see if overall economic activity has actually slowed down. For example, the rate of **new business capital formation** might be considered, as might **capacity utilization** in the manufacturing sector. Capacity utilization is the degree to which the available stock of business capital is being used in actual production.

As it turns out, the official designator of the reference dates for the beginning and ending of recessions takes into account all the different bits of aggregate information we have on the functioning of the economy. The National Bureau of Economic Research, a nonprofit organization, designates the dates of recessions that are used for official purposes. By measuring the things previously mentioned and innumerable others, its elaborate system comes up with a more or less accurate date for when the recession began and when it ended.

Incidentally, the National Bureau of Economic Research defines a recession as *three* consecutive quarters of falling real GNP. At the moment, most economists settle for this definition. As long as it is understood that even the official reference dates given by the National Bureau are arbitrary, there is no harm in using its dating for recessions. However, because there are no theoretical underpinnings for arbitrarily determining the operational definition of a recession, or even of a depression, we should be somewhat circumspect about placing much emphasis on the exact dating of particular phases of the business cycle.

Summary

Any definition of a recession must, by necessity, be arbitrary. In general, we define a recession as a period during which the economy is not growing as rapidly as it normally has over the past hundred years or so. The National Bureau of Economic Research officially declares a recession when there are three consecutive quarters of falling real GNP.

Discussion Questions

1. Why is it important to know the exact date of the start of a recession?

2. If we were to enter a long period during which there was no economic growth—increase in real GNP—would the National Bureau of Economic Research have to change its official definition of a recession?

On Measuring Unemployment and Full Employment

Key Terms

labor force The number of individuals over sixteen years of age who are not in school, not engaged in home housework, not voluntarily idle, or retired, and are either working or looking for a job.

real wage rate The wage rate corrected for inflation.

average duration of unemployment The average number of weeks that the average unemployed person remains unemployed before finding a new job.

The **labor force** in this country is huge, some 114 million members. At various times, however, millions of those in the labor force are counted as unemployed. To a great extent the unemployment rate determines how policy makers feel about the level of total economic activity. When the unemployment rate starts creeping up, Washington officials get worried, as do those who are unemployed; the latter who also sometimes get agitated and demonstrate in disorderly ways. Those who are still working but in danger of losing their jobs if the economy softens are also worried. Along with the annual rate of inflation, the percentage rate of unemployment is the most closely watched indicator of economic well-being that we have.

The U.S. Bureau of the Census and the Bureau of Labor Statistics (BLS) compile data on the size of the labor force and the number of unemployed. Counted in the civilian labor force are individuals over sixteen years of age and not in the military, prisons, homes for the aged, or mental institutions. Retired people, some seasonal workers, and students are also excluded from the labor force, as are the unemployed *not* seeking work. The estimated unemployment rate is one of the statistics that comes out of the monthly Current Population Survey (CPS), undertaken jointly by the Bureau of the Census and the Bureau of Labor Statistics. Because, as you might expect, the survey cannot contact every adult in the country, statisticians have designed a sampling method to collect these data. The United States is divided into about 2,000 "primary sampling units," the bulk of which consists of a single county or a number of contiguous counties. Presumably, each sampling unit contains a mixture of urban and rural residents, low- and high-income earners, and a variety of occupations and industries.

Each sampling unit is further subdivided into 461 areas, called strata, according to characteristics like rate of growth, population density, and principal industries. From each primary sampling unit, statisticians select one stratum to represent the entire unit. Within that stratum, a number of individual households is randomly selected to be contacted during the monthly survey. A certain proportion of the households is changed each month to reduce any biased answers that might develop in a particular household that is interviewed month after month. On the second or third Monday of each month, well over 1,000 employees of the Census Bureau take their blank questionnaires to about 50,000 household units. The unemployed are determined from these completed questionnaires.

A person is considered unemployed if he or she did not work at all during the survey week but was available for work; was looking for work; was waiting to be called back to a job from which he or she was laid off; was waiting to start a new job within the next month and was not in school; or was temporarily ill and otherwise would have been looking for a job.

Government statisticians have not always followed these rules. For example, during the Great Depression (1933–1941) official unemployment rates ranged from almost twenty-five percent in 1933 to about ten percent in 1941. However, these data are deceiving because they include as unemployed the approximately 4 million workers in such government programs as the Civilian Conservation Corps and the Works Progress Administration. Why? It was reasoned that because the government jobs were not permanent, the private sector would eventually have to provide job openings to take care of these 4 million individuals. Because these people were working, the true unemployment rate during that period would have been approximately four to seven percent lower than that reported by the BLS.

Although today's unemployment statistics are not altered in such ways, there are, nevertheless, economists who think current official data are misleading. Many critics of the way unemployment is measured contend that, particularly during periods of recession, such as 1969 to 1970, 1973 to 1975 and 1981 to 1982, unemployment statistics grossly underestimated the true amount of unemployment. Why? Because of the "hidden" unemployment that results when discouraged workers leave the labor force. During a recession, increasing numbers of those in the labor force gradually drop out because they are discouraged. They no longer think it is worthwhile looking, or they fear they could never get a job, or they are just "sitting it out" until a business upturn occurs. It was not uncommon during the last recession for union leaders to contend that the true unemployment rate was several percentage points higher than the government statistics showed.

Perhaps this was so, but an alternative view of unemployment suggests otherwise. If we treat labor like any other resource, we expect that a larger quantity will be supplied at higher prices.[1] Thus, if the resource called labor is similar to other resources, when its price (that is, **real wage rate**) either rises less than expected or actually falls during a recession, we would predict that a smaller quantity would be forthcoming from suppliers. Thus, we would predict that during recessions the labor force would contract; hence, it might be appropriate to ignore, at least to some extent, the question of "hidden" unemployment that is caused by discouraged workers leaving the labor force.

Still other areas of ambiguity can be found in the unemployment statistics, such as in the length of time workers remain unemployed. For example, the *rate* of unemployment can rise even when the absolute number of workers *becoming* unemployed per week remains constant. This occurs whenever the **average duration of unemployment** increases since more workers do not then leave the ranks of the unemployed. Hence, an increase by a week or two in the average duration of unemployment may increase the unemployment rate by half a percentage point. For policy purposes, perhaps a better statistic to look at is the percentage of the unemployed labor force that remains out of work for a long period of time—say, more than six months. It turns out that even during severe recessions the bulk of unemployed workers found a job within fourteen weeks. Moreover, not all unemployment consists of workers who were fired or laid off: About half of those reported as unemployed had either voluntarily left their last job, never worked before, or were reentering the labor force after an absence due to illness or pregnancy, for example.

We must also realize that the survey methods used to collect data produce an upward bias in the U.S. unemployment statistic; that is, the methods have a built-in tendency to exaggerate the

---

[1] The supply curve of labor is upward sloping.

statistic. The main question asked of someone out of work is, "Are you looking for work?" An affirmative response is considered acceptable even if that person merely flips through the local newspaper job-vacancy columns three minutes a night. In the United Kingdom, unemployed workers must report that they are unemployed. Thus, a U.S. unemployment rate of, say, six percent might be equivalent to a United Kingdom unemployment rate of three percent.

Of course, looking for work is not the only criterion required for someone to be counted as unemployed. The other two key elements that determine whether an individual survey is counted as unemployed are (1) not working and (2) being available for work. These two requirements are satisfied by registering for work as a part of the eligibility for certain types of welfare assistance programs. For example, recipients of food stamps, Aid to Families with Dependent Children (AFDC), and several other smaller federal assistance programs are required to register for work as a condition of eligibility. Specifically, by the terms of the 1971 and 1977 amendments to the Food Stamp and AFDC program legislation, certain recipients must register for employment with state employment services offices at the time of application and at least once every six months thereafter. Of course, any welfare recipient who has registered for work can lose his or her welfare assistance by refusing to comply with employee service directives, such as requests for testing, counseling, and so on. In fact, though, only six percent of the food stamp registrants, for example, have been declared ineligible for benefits because of their failure to comply with work registration provisions or with employee service directives. The end result of the requirement that certain welfare recipients must register for work is an upward bias in measured unemployment statistics. In 1977, for example, over 2 million individuals registered to work under the Food Stamp and AFDC programs. To determine the extent to which such registrations constitute an overcounting of unemployment, we must find out how many welfare recipients who do register are unemployable or have no need or intention to work.

Now consider the elusive notion of "full emloyment." Looking at the average duration of unemployment over a long period of time, so that in some sense we can call that number "normal," we can derive perhaps a suitable theoretical notion of full employment. Full employment would then prevail when waiting times were "average" or "normal," and less-than-full employment would exist when waiting times between jobs were greater than "average." Less than "average" waiting times between jobs would in turn be considered "over" full employment, which occurs when workers take jobs that pay less "on average" than they would have obtained had they waited an optimum—that is, average—length of time before they found a new job. In this view, unemployment figures differ from the average long-run normal because workers are insufficiently informed about market conditions and seek out wages that are either too high or too low. We will treat this important topic again in chapter 26 when we examine the conditions necessary for high rates of unemployment to coexist with high rates of inflation.

Whatever the appropriate measure of unemployment might be, some "normal" measured rate of unemployment is used to define full employment. It is interesting to note that, prior to the Great Depression, there was no such concept as full employment. Economists prior to the Depression accepted full employment as "automatic." John Maynard Keynes, in his *General Theory of Employment, Interest, and Money* (1936), brought the expression into widespread use. In the 1944 presidential campaign, both major party platforms advocated the attainment of full employment, although neither party quantified the term. Later that year, however, in a Congressional study, full employment was defined in terms of the *absolute number* of unemployed, which was set at 2 million.

The notion of "maximum" (which presumably meant "full") employment was incorporated in the Employment Act, authored by Senator James E. Murray in 1945 and passed in 1946. The Act came to be known as the Full Employment Act. The first official federal quantification of the concept of full employment was included in the 1947 *Economic Report of the President*; 2 million persons unemployed was "close to the minimum unavoidable in a free economy of great mobility such as ours." By the 1950s, the Council of Economic Advisers and the Joint Economic Committee of Congress declared 3.6 to 4 percent unemployment to be the full-employment level. Four percent stuck for quite a while. The Council of Economic Advisers in the 1960s considered it an "interim goal of public policy." However, those who were members of the council during the early 1960s will be quick to admit that no objective means were used to come up with the figure. It was somehow considered, by "consensus," an acceptable level of unemployment.

In the past few years, particularly because the unemployment rate has rarely dropped to close to four percent, government policy makers have questioned what the "true" full-employment rate of unemployment is. Now the government appears satisfied with six percent as the acceptable level. Can anything favor increasing what is deemed the full-employment level of unemployment? Proponents of increasing the official full employment rate of unemployment contend that because there is more friction in our economy as it becomes more complex, we should expect more people to stay out of jobs longer as they take more time to acquire more complicated bits of information on where job availabilities are greatest. Furthermore, it is contended that because of the change in the age/sex makeup of the labor force, we would expect normally higher rates of unemployment. For example, teenagers over sixteen years now constitute a larger portion of the labor force, and they have always had higher rates of unemployment.

However full employment is defined, we must always remember that that definition is essentially ad hoc. Policy makers should realize this when they affix specific policy recommendations to particular changes in the employment rate. Moreover, they must realize that some of their policy making may lead not to reductions in unemployment but, rather, to permanent increases—a phenomenon we examine in the next chapter.

Summary

The unemployment rate is determined first by finding the size of the total labor force and then by dividing that number into an estimate of the number of unemployed. That estimate is found through monthly sampling throughout the country. Some argue that the sampling techniques underestimate true unemployment because of discouraged workers. Others argue that it is not the *rate* of unemployment but the average *duration* of unemployment that is important, since we should only be concerned with those who remain unemployed for long periods of time. Perhaps several million individuals are officially counted as unemployed because they are required to register for work in order to obtain food stamps and Aid to Families with Dependent Children even though they have no intention of obtaining a job.

One notion of full employment would be that any time the average duration of unemployment is greater than what is normal, we are not at the full employment rate of unemployment. Whatever measure of the full employment rate of unemployment is accepted be it four percent, five percent, or six percent, that measure is arbitrary.

Discussion Questions

1. What does it mean to say that the government's measure of the full employment rate of unemployment is arbitrary?

2. Why shouldn't discouraged workers also be included as unemployed, even though when sampled they indicate that they are not looking for a job?

The New Unemployment

Key Terms

experience ratings Ratings applied to different firms according to past experience with the number of workers they fired or laid off. In other words, experience ratings refer to the employment variability record of each employer.

law of demand The inverse relationship between the quantity demanded and the price, other things being held constant.

implicit marginal tax rate The effective marginal tax rate facing an individual who will lose unemployment benefits and other transfer payments if that individual goes back to work.

empirical question A question that can only be answered by looking at the facts—actual data on past events.

During some years in the 1970s and 1980s, unemployed workers received unemployment benefits that sometimes exceeded a total of $1 billion per month. Under our system of unemployment insurance and compensation, eligible workers are provided with direct transfer payments from their state unemployment offices.

Since the late 1960s, the average rate of unemployment has been rising intermittently. Perhaps this is caused by structural changes in the labor force or a more complicated job market, reasons cited in the last chapter. However, a number of researchers are now linking our system of unemployment compensation to what they call the "new unemployment"—that is, unemployment *caused* by unemployment compensation. How could unemployment compensation cause unemployment? On a theoretical level, the answer is not hard to find because it is directly related to the quantity of leisure demanded by individual workers.

It appears that unemployment compensation has an important effect on the amount of temporary layoffs in our employment system. About half the adults unemployed at any time have been laid off. Among men twenty-four to sixty-four years old, this fraction rises to nearly three-fourths. A surprisingly large percent of this group of individuals is rehired after only a temporary spell of unemployment. Some studies show that the amount of rehiring is between seventy to eighty percent! How does unemployment compensation affect the amount of temporary layoffs? It all has to do with the fact that there is an imperfect relationship between an employer's contribution to the total unemployment insurance fund and the amount of fluctuation in that employer's total number of workers. In other words, an employer who has a large amount of temporary layoffs does not pay, or contribute, a proportionately higher number of dollars into the fund than an employer who has virtually no temporary layoffs (a stable labor force).

Firms pay taxes of about one percent of their payroll toward unemployment insurance even if they have no layoffs. On the other hand, they pay no more than five percent even if they have more layoffs than another employer. Thus, employers who frequently lay off workers have most of the resulting expense of unemployment benefits subsidized, at least in part, by those employers who do not lay off workers. Individuals will accept jobs more readily with high probabilities of layoffs if they know they will obtain unemployment benefits.

Thus, the current unemployment insurance system imposes an efficiency loss by causing firms to lay off more workers than they would otherwise. The solution would be to impose full employer **experience ratings** so that employers who laid off large numbers of employees would have to bear a proportionate increase in their unemloyment insurance contributions.

Many critics of the unemployment insurance system have pointed out that the nontaxable nature of its benefits is more beneficial to individuals in higher marginal tax brackets. Thus, the individual who is the second wage earner in a family where the working partner is already making $25,000 a year will save more taxes because of the tax-free nature of unemployment benefits than someone in a family making only $10,000 a year. The solution, obviously, is to tax unemployment insurance benefits. Not only would taxing unemployment benefits leave relatively untouched the benefits received by very poor families (because they are in a very low or zero marginal tax bracket), but it would serve to increase the price of leisure for those high-income families now drawing unemployment benefits. Hence, unemployed workers in those families would react by shortening their average duration of unemployment. Congress has already taken steps in this direction: the 1978 Revenue Act included a provision that, under some circumstances, imposes a tax on unemployment compensation.

If we consider leisure a good that is scarce and desirable, we assume that it follows the **law of demand**—that is, the quantity demanded will be inversely related to its price. What is the price of leisure? It is the value of the highest foregone alternative. Generally, we measure the (opportunity) cost or price of leisure by the real wages given up by *not* working. Now, we must be careful to calculate the price of leisure at the take-home income figure. That is, when you decide not to work one week (assuming you are working), the price of the leisure that you are "buying" is not your *gross* pay, but, rather, your *net* (after-tax) paycheck. The hourly price of leisure, then, can be approximated by an individual's net, after-tax, hourly real wage rate.

What does this have to do with unemployment compensation? A lot, because when workers become unemployed—that is, have more leisure—the price they pay for that unemployment (leisure time) depends on whether or not they obtain unemployment compensation benefits. Moreover, their net take-home pay when they were working must be compared with the net amount they receive not only from unemployment compensation benefits but from whatever other transfers they might get, such as food stamps, housing supplements, medical insurance premiums, supplemental unemployment benefits (SUB), and so on.

The actual income of unemployed workers with SUBs, unemployment compensation, and related benefits, especially food stamps, can be as high as ninety-five percent of normal after-tax earnings. Given that work-related expenses, such as the cost of transportation and tools, are not required by those who are unemployed, some workers find that they would gain little or nothing by going back to work before their unemployment benefits run out. Basically, that means that some individuals face a very high **implicit marginal tax rate** if they decide to return to work before their benefits expire. If, for example, they can obtain eighty percent of their after-tax income from unemployment and other related benefits, then returning to work while they are still eligible for these benefits means they will face an eighty percent marginal tax rate. There's another way to state this in terms of the price of leisure: since the price of leisure is the price of after-tax income lost, the unemployed worker receiving the benefits just mentioned faces an opportunity cost of leisure of only twenty percent of his or her take-home pay.

Leisure has become a relatively cheaper commodity. Economists predict, therefore, that more will be demanded. An additional effect of unemployment compensation is that it reduces the incentives for the unemployed to take jobs for which they are "overtrained." For example, an unemployed high school social studies teacher may refuse to become a secretary or a shipping dock supervisor so long as unemployment benefits last.

To what extent unemployment compensation affects the rate of unemployment is an **empirical question**, one that only the data can answer. A number of researchers have studied the question and have come up with varying estimates—from a high of about 2 percentage points of unemployment due to unemployment compensation down to a low of 0.7 percentage points. Here we are talking about measured unemployment. It is quite another matter to determine the effect that unemployment compensation has on total, economywide production. Some researchers contend that, during recessions, much of the increased unemployment due to unemployment compensation is merely a shift of people who would have been out of the labor force to the status of unemployed; thus, the resource loss is slight.

Summary

Unemployment compensation may lead to higher normal levels of unemployment for a variety of reasons. Because employers are not assessed an unemployment insurance contribution that varies proportionally with the variability in employment, those employers who have high variability of employment are being subsidized by those employers with low variability of employment. Unemployment insurance benefits are typically not taxed, and therefore represent a greater benefit to families with two income earners in higher marginal tax brackets. Full taxation of unemployment benefits would alter this situation. The existence of unemployment insurance increases the quantity of leisure demanded (or the average duration of unemployment) because it reduces the opportunity cost of taking longer to find a job. Alternatively, one can look at the existence of unemployment and other transfer benefits as imposing a high implicit marginal tax rate on workers who decide to go back to work prior to using up their available unemployment benefits.

Discussion Questions

1. Is there any way to have an unemployment compensation system that does not lead to an increase in the average duration of unemployment?

2. What arguments are there against taxing unemployment benefits?

Profits
and How
to Measure
Them

Key Terms

national product The sum total of the value of the output of final goods and services produced in one year in an economy.

net worth The difference between assets and liabilities, or the difference between what is owned and what is owed.

inventory profits The increase in the market value of inventories of finished goods owned by a company.

cash flow The difference between actual cash receipts and actual cash outlays of a firm.

accounting profits The difference between total revenues and all explicit costs.

economic profits The difference between total revenues and all costs, including the opportunity cost of all resources used in the production process.

"Profits Up 55 Percent over Last Year." "Oil Companies Make Obscene Profits—Up 126%." "Profit Inflation Proceeds Full Speed Ahead." These are some examples of newspaper headlines that emphasize the large profits American corporations have been making. However, if we look at profits dispassionately, we see a less rosy picture of what they now are, have been, and are likely to be. In the first place, a distinction must be made between absolute profits and the profit rate. Three percent of a $1-billion capital investment is a lot of money, but it's an awfully low profit rate. As corporations and the economy have both increased in size, absolute profits naturally become larger. They may look obscene to an unknowledgeable observer merely because such large numbers are involved.

In the second place, although after-tax profits appear to have been rising over time, correcting for the impact of inflation reveals that the upward trend in profits is far less dramatic. After all, from 1950 to 1975 the Consumer Price Index rose by 225 percent, while profits, after taxes, rose only 300 percent. In terms of real purchasing power, after-tax profits rose only by 75 percent for the two-and-a-half decades after the Korean conflict, or at an average annual rate of less than 3 percent.

Moreover, in the last fifty years, the owners of capital have not increased their share of national income. Compensation to employees has varied between sixty-five and seventy-five percent over this period so that the remainder for owners of capital—profits, rent, and interest—has stayed at around twenty-five to thirty-five percent.

Perhaps more revealing is the division of **national product** between profits and wages. Here cyclical fluctuations are even more pronounced. The ratio of after-tax profits for nonfinancial corporations to wages has fallen dramatically in the last recessions. For example, in the 1969 to 1971 recession, this ratio was 0.07, compared to a ratio of almost 0.17 five years earlier at the beginning of the Vietnam conflict. Why does this variation occur? It occurs partly because the compensation of employees does not fall as dramatically as after-tax profits during business downturns. Because employers are uncertain about how long a recession will last and how severe it will be, they prefer to keep on workers quite far into a recession to hedge against the cost of firing and then hiring workers when business improves. In a sense, labor is a quasi-fixed factor of production; put another way, firms choose to keep on hand inventories of labor during business downturns. We would, therefore, expect that as business slacks off and revenues decrease, total wages will not fall as much as profits. Thus, the ratio of profits to wages will fall because profits are a *residual*—what remains after all expenses are paid.

How is a rising ratio of profits to wages related to price inflation? In most periods when the profit share in the manufacturing section has risen rapidly, the increases in output prices have been relatively moderate. In fact, if we closely examine many business upturns, we find that, when output-price rises accelerate, the profit share actually begins to fall.

In any event, profit statements given in newspaper and magazine articles are often misleading. A dollar figure is often given instead of a percentage of investment. For example, being told that the profits of XYZ Corporation were $100 million gives you no information. Is that company highly profitable, or not very profitable? The only way you can find out is to compare the profits to the **net worth** of the company. If the net worth of the company is $500 million, then its' rate of return is twenty percent, and that is usually considered a pretty good profit. But what if the XYZ Corporation has a net worth of $2 billion. $100 million is only five percent of $2 billion and that is a relatively low rate or return.

Simple before-tax dollar profit figures also ignore increased taxes that corporations have had to pay during the 1970s and 1980s because of fictitious **inventory profits.** That is, firms have been forced to restate the market value of the inventories of goods they own because inflation raises the price for which they can sell those goods. These inventory revaluations show fictitious profits because the firm is no better off if it disposes of the appreciated inventory since it must replace that inventory at higher prices. In other words, inventory profits provide no **cash flow** for new plant and equipment expansion or for dividends. Nonetheless, Uncle Sam imposes a profits tax on such profits. Thus, the difference between gross profits and after-tax profits has been widening as inflation has caused firms to pay ever-increasing taxes on their inventory profits.

Whatever one's view might be on the "obscenity of profits," it must be recognized that profits perform a basic function in the American economy: They direct resources to their highest-valued use. Moreover, a significant portion of the profits in any industry is merely the opportunity cost of capital—that is, the rate of return to invested capital necessary to keep that capital in its present activity. **Accounting profits**—the difference between total revenues and explicit costs—grossly overstate what are called pure **economic profits**—the difference between total revenue and the full opportunity cost of all factors of production. The lure of pure economic profits induces entrepreneurs to take more risks. Once this lure is eliminated, risk taking will be reduced. This will become increasingly obvious in the future as it becomes more and more politically unwise to earn above-normal profits no matter what the situation.

To take a specific example, consider the case of the United States oil companies during the 1973–74 oil crisis. Because of the oil embargo, the United States presumably suffered a reduction in the supply of foreign oil. As one might expect, when an alternative supply of a resource is eliminated, the owners of extant supplies will earn higher-than-normal rates of return. When the supply is reduced and the demand remains relatively stable, prices rise, and owners of resources still in the industry earn pure economic profits. However, when this happened to the oil companies during the crisis, their higher profits were called "obscene" by people like Senator Henry Jackson (Dem., Washington). But it is the possibility of making such high profits that would induce oil companies to take the risk of providing extra capacity or reserves for future periods of oil shortages. That is, if relatively high profits can be made by selling oil during oil shortages, then more entrepreneurs will be willing to keep inventories of oil or oil-producing and refining capacity—something they otherwise would not do. However, in a future oil shortage (whatever its cause), "obscene" profits may be even less politically acceptable than they were a few years ago. Knowing that, the oil industry has less incentive to take a chance on keeping capital tied up in providing for the next emergency. When that time comes, the additional returns will be insufficient to cover storage costs.

Summary

A simple absolute dollar figure on profits alone does not yield much useful information. That dollar figure at a minimum should be corrected for price changes and taxes the corporation pays. Additionally, even price-corrected after-tax profits do not reveal the rate of return to investment. One must divide the company's net worth into price-corrected after-tax profits to get the real after-tax rate of return to investment. Profits perform the function of directing resources to their highest value used in a market economy. When profits are not allowed to perform this function, an alternative resource-allocating device must be substituted.

Discussion Questions

1. What is the difference between rate of return to investment and rate of return to sales?

2. Who would be interested in distinguishing between accounting profits and economic profits?

PART THREE

The
Keynesian
Model,
Fiscal Policy,
and the
Public Debt

Are We Saving Enough?

Key Terms

personal saving That part of disposable personal income that households do not consume per year.

disposable income Income available either to spend or save after all taxes are paid.

rate of saving The percentage of income that is not consumed (spent) over a one-year period.

gross private saving Personal saving plus business saving.

depreciation The wearing out of capital equipment due to use and age, and the reduction in the value of capital equipment due to obsolescence.

At the beginning of the 1980s, the ratio of **personal saving** to **disposable** (after-tax) **income** in the United States hit an all-time low. It was a little higher than 4.5 percent, the lowest figure in the past quarter century. Compared to the rest of the world, the United States saving rate is indeed paltry.

Other countries have attempted to improve their **rate of saving** in the private sector in a number of ways. West Germany, for example, adds a bonus to special savings accounts that are frozen for six to seven years. Certain lower-income individuals can deposit around $500 a year into such an account and earn, on top of regular interest, a tax-free government-provided bonus of 14 percent a year, plus 2 percent for each dependent child. Employees can set up special seven-year accounts by authorizing regular payroll deductions of up to around $400 a year. These special accounts qualify for a government bonus of 30 to 40 percent per year. In France individuals can earn tax-free interest of 7.5 percent on deposits of up to about $10,000 in mutual savings banks. The first $1,000 of income from government bonds is also tax free, as is the first $700 of dividend income from stocks. In Japan things are even better. Virtually all interest income earned by the average Japanese citizens is exempt from taxes. As much as $60,000 in savings can be shielded from taxes on interest income.

The results seem to be in line with our expectations. Japan, France, and West Germany save a much higher percentage of disposable after-tax income than the United States. For example, at the beginning of this decade, the percentage of disposable personal income allocated to saving was 20 percent in Japan, 17 percent in France, and 14 percent in West Germany. Compare these numbers with the 4.5 percent in the United States.

The numbers on personal saving in the United States do not tell the whole story, however. Yes, it is true that the personal saving rate has varied from a low of about 4 percent to a high of about 7.7 percent over the last thirty-five years. On the other hand, the **gross private saving** rate has stayed constant at around 15.5 percent over that same time period. Gross private saving is a true measure of total saving in the economy.

Personal saving represents a relatively small part of gross private saving. The remainder consists of business saving; that is, the amounts that firms set aside for the **depreciation** of their capital equipment, plus all of the profits that they retain rather than pay out to shareholders. Business saving makes up about four-fifths of total savings.

In the United States the gross private saving rate varies hardly at all across time. The difference between the highest and lowest average for the gross private saving rate was only .2 percentage points from 1954 to 1980. This is a relatively insignificant amount compared to the long-term average of 15.8 percent. Indeed, the gross private saving rate has been relatively constant for more than a quarter of a century; in terms of long-run U.S. saving behavior, it has not changed significantly in the last hundred years. The U.S. economy today saves about the same fraction of GNP that it did before the turn of the century.

Summary

The personal saving rate in the United States is relatively low, by both international and historical standards. Other countries create tax incentives to induce private individuals to save a larger percentage of their disposable income. The data on personal private saving in the United States, however, do not tell the entire story. Gross private saving in this country has averaged around 15.5 percent over the last thirty-five years. Corporations have filled in whenever private individuals have reduced their saving rate. Indeed, business saving makes up about four-fifths of total saving.

Discussion Questions

1. What would be the effect of total tax exemption on all interest from private savings?

2. If the U.S. government undertook efforts to boost private personal saving, how would consumers "pay" for any increase in saving?

13

Social Security and Saving

Key Term

income transfer program A program in which some individuals are taxed in order to give benefits in the form of money income or in-kind transfers to other individuals.

During the Depression, it was evident that many people had not provided for themselves in case of emergencies. An especially large percentage of the elderly population, which could not rely on its children for support, became destitute. To prevent a recurrence of so much pain and suffering by elderly people, Congress passed the Social Security Act of 1935. By January 1940, when the first monthly benefit started, only 22,000 people received payments. Today, however, well over ninety-two percent of people sixty-five or older receive Social Security benefits—or *could* receive them if they weren't still working. If our population growth continues to slow down, the average age of the population will continue to rise. Hence, the number of people eligible for and receiving Social Security will increase as a percentage of the total population.

The Social Security system is basically an *involuntary* benefit program; that is, if we work, we *must* participate in the Social Security program. Even self-employed people must pay self-employment Social Security taxes. If you work for someone else your employer must file Social Security taxes for you. Of the people earning money in the United States, ninety-five percent contribute to Social Security. According to supporters of the program, Social Security is obligatory in order to ensure that all older Americans will have at least a basic living income and won't need welfare payments.

The Social Security Act, sometimes called the OASDHI, provides benefits for old-age retirement, survivors, disability, and health insurance. It is essentially an **income transfer program,** financed by compulsory payroll taxes levied on both employers and employees; those who are employed transfer income to those who are retired or disabled. One pays for Social Security for others while working and usually receives benefits after retirement. The benefit payments usually are made to those reaching retirement age. Also, when an insured worker dies, benefits accrue to his or her survivors. Special benefits provide for disabled workers. Additionally, Social Security now provides for Medicare. The Social Security Act of 1935 also provided for the establishment of an unemployment insurance system.

In the last few years, we have seen a series of alarming articles and exposés on the supposed future bankruptcy of the Social Security system. Americans, particularly older ones, were shocked to find out that the Social Security system only had enough money in its trust funds to cover slightly more than one-half of the total benefits paid in any one year to recipients. In essence, everyone was saying that the Social Security system was not actuarially sound. After all, a private insurance program must, by law, have a trust fund that at any moment could finance all the benefits promised to its members. But the benefits owed members of the Social Security system are valued anywhere from $3.5 to $5 trillion!

The original system was sound, however. Federal Insurance Contributions Act (FICA) collections started in 1937, but benefits were delayed until 1940. The tax rate at the beginning was 2 percent—1 percent on both employer and employee on the first $3,000 of income. Since no one received any benefits for three years, the trust fund became sizable. Thus, although the Social Security tax was supposed to increase in 1940, it did not. In fact, it wasn't until 1950 that it rose to 3 percent (1.5 percent on each party). Since then, coverage has expanded greatly, as well as the size of benefits. Social, economic, and political pressures have escalated benefits to levels never dreamed of in 1940. Checks then were as little as $10.00 per month, $41.20 at the most. By the beginning of the 1980s, the minimum was $133.90, and the maximum $587.70 per month for a man retiring at age sixty-five. On the other side of the coin, taxes paid have skyrocketed. When the system started, the typical collection was $30.00. By 1965, the maximum any worker could pay was only $174. By 1982, the maximum had jumped to $2,130, with the employer contributing an equal amount. Clearly, those who got in on the ground floor of the Social Security program got a good deal; they've been receiving benefits greatly in excess of what they paid in taxes.

The system is not bankrupt today, in spite of what the media tell us. It can't be because it's a transfer system, not an insurance system. Those who are working today are paying taxes to finance retirement payments to those who are no longer working. It's a pay-as-you-go system. Thus, as long as Congress is willing to tax sufficiently to pay for the benefits, Social Security benefits will always be paid. Indeed, the notion that the Social Security system may be heading toward bankruptcy is a bit of a red herring. Perhaps more important is the effect of an ever-increasing Social Security tax on the rate of private saving.

According to some economists, high Social Security tax rates coupled with high benefits are causing a significant reduction in private saving. Today, the average married male worker retires with Social Security benefits for himself and his wife that replace eighty percent of his maximum *after-tax* earnings. For what reason, therefore, should the typical worker save a large amount for his or her retirement? In other words, what reason is there for the average American worker to forego current consumption in order to save more in a private pension plan? Consider the fact that in 1978 Social Security payments exceeded $100 billion, which exceeded more than all private saving, including that done by corporations. Some researchers believe that the Social Security system reduces private saving by one-third of what it would otherwise be. And the system does nothing to offset this lower rate of saving.

A private pension plan takes an individual's funds and invests them—puts them back into the economy where they are used for expansion of industry and the like. The Social Security system, as we mentioned, is financed on a pay-as-you-go basis. All the tax dollars collected today are immediately paid out today. Thus, the system does virtually no saving itself. And the reduction in private saving due to Social Security taxes and benefits without any offsetting increase in the program leads to a lower rate of saving and less capital formation than would otherwise be. It is perhaps, at least in part, because of Social Security that, since 1960, the United States has had a personal saving rate of about one-half the average personal saving rate of all the other industrial nations in the world. Since existing legislation calls for rapid increases in future Social Security benefits and ever-increasing Social Security taxes, it is conceivable that the personal saving rate in the United States may fall even lower. It is not surprising that many economists have called for a reduction in the growth of Social Security benefits. In order to protect those who rely on such benefits, there would be no reduction in existing benefits. If this reduced growth of benefits were publicly announced, the rate of private saving might increase. Individuals would rely more on private pensions and their own saving plans. This perhaps would increase capital formation and promote a greater rate of economic growth and a higher standard of living in the future.

There is another side to this argument, however. Individuals who reduce their private saving because of promised Social Security benefits in the future are essentially accepting the consequent reduced rate of capital formation, reduced economic growth, and reduced potential higher living standards. If individuals had perfect foresight, though, they would not reduce private saving merely because of the proffered Social Security benefits. Instead, they would know that, as a nation, we would have a lower standard of living than otherwise because of all of this reduced private saving. To the extent that individuals do act *as if* they understood this rather subtle argument, private saving rates are not and will not be affected by increasing Social Security benefits. Then the concern simply becomes one of deciding how much income we wish to transfer to nonworking, older people and what effect any increased taxes necessary to pay for higher benefits will have on individuals' incentives to work.

Summary

The Social Security system is essentially a pay-as-you-go transfer system. Income is transferred from those who work to those who are not working (i.e., retired). Social Security is not an insurance system. It is unlikely to go bankrupt because there is always the taxing power of the federal government available to pay for legislated benefits. The existence of Social Security retirement benefits may, however, be reducing the personal saving rate in the United States. Some economists argue that this reduction in personal saving has led to slower economic growth.

Discussion Questions

1. What is the difference between a private pension plan and the Social Security system?

2. Is it possible that Congress can continuously increase Social Security benefits faster than the rate of economic growth?

Can the Government Create Jobs Directly?

Key Terms

monetary policy Changes in the rate of growth of the money supply in circulation and/or credit market conditions by the Federal Reserve System.

fiscal policy Deliberate changes in the rate of government spending or taxation made by the president and Congress.

demand curve A graphic representation showing planned purchase rates at different prices other things held constant.

displacement effect When applied to federal funding of public jobs, the displacement of the use of state and local funds for those same jobs.

countercyclical measure The use of government policy tools to counter the ups and downs in business activity resulting from the business cycle.

job vouchers A voucher the recipient of which could use with any employer of his or her choice. The employer receiving the voucher would be reimbursed by the government for all or part of the worker's salary.

The major stabilizing tools at the government's disposal consist of **monetary policy** and **fiscal policy.** The former depends on actions of the Federal Reserve. The latter depends on, to a large extent, actions of Congress in changing government spending and/or taxation. Starting in the 1930s during the depths of the Great Depression, the federal government attempted to create jobs directly by instituting federal job creation programs. Work relief and public works programs reached their peak in 1938 when the federal government employed nearly four million workers. The government certainly believed that these four million workers would not have received jobs otherwise because they were not removed from the official unemployment statistics.

The urban riots of the 1960s and the high unemployment rates in the 1970s and early 1980s stimulated interest in direct federal job creation. During the 1970s almost twenty federal jobs programs were put into operation. These involved direct job creation as well as training projects. In 1973 the Comprehensive Employment and Training Act (CETA) consolidated all such efforts. Under CETA federal dollars were channeled to county and city governments that became responsible for providing job opportunities and training. The onset of the CETA programs were aimed at solving structural unemployment problems. This was evidenced by the training and work experience program emphasis at that time. By 1975, however, the emphasis shifted to direct job creation. At the peak of the public service employment effort, about three-quarters of a million jobs had been created by CETA subsidies.

The Reagan administration made attempts to reduce the budget of these programs significantly. Cries of despair were heard around the nation, particularly when the unemployment rate hit almost ten percent by the summer of 1982. Proponents of jobs program argue that CETA and other types of job creation programs *can* work. After all, according to these proponents, the labor market is segmented, and skilled workers don't have to worry. Movements in wage rates clear the market for their skills. But unskilled workers are another story. Certain market imperfections keep wages artificially high, leading to relatively permanent levels of involuntary unemployment. In step public service jobs; they can reduce the unemployment of these unskilled workers without creating pressure on wages. All that government officials need do is to identify and hire those workers who cannot get jobs at the prevailing wage. Jobs can be created by circumventing the market imperfection that leads to this permanent class of unemployed.

Critics of job creation programs reject the notion of a segmented labor market. They contend that labor market imperfections are unimportant, so unimportant that they do not influence the unemployment rate. How can these critics of job creation programs explain such high rates of unemployment among unskilled workers? They do so by claiming that high job turnover rates are inherent in these markets. In essence, then, they are saying that the wages of unskilled workers clear the market. There is no permanent class of unemployed unskilled workers. Any job creation program would thereby only increase wages paid for those workers. The quantity of unskilled workers demanded would fall in the private sector (after all, the **demand curve** for unskilled labor slopes downward). The extreme critics of job creation programs contend that the programs simply are a financial "wash"—the increase in public sector employment is matched by a similar decrease in private sector employment

Another criticism of public jobs has to do with the **displacement effect.** Federal funds may simply displace state and local government funds.

As we pointed out before, since CETA most public jobs programs are administered through grants to state and local agencies. New job positions are supposed to be created and new workers hired, particularly from an unemployment group targeted. However, given the difficulty of monitoring the use of federal funds, it is indeed possible for state and local agencies merely to substitute the federal funds for funds they would have spent otherwise. In the extreme, if the displacement rate were 100 percent, public jobs programs would not have any net impact on wages, employment, or expenditures. The only effect would be to shift the burden of financing the services provided by the state and local agencies from state and local taxpayers to all federal taxpayers.

Moving now from the broader issue of the net employment effect, what can be said about satisfying the more specific objective of ameliorating the employment problems of low-skilled workers? If we look at the experience of the Public Employment Program (PEP) started in 1971, we find that only seventeen percent of the workers hired actually satisfied the official criteria of "disadvantaged." The educational level of those employees hired under the program was on average greater than the work force as a whole. According to two researchers examining the program, George Johnson and James Tomola,[1] the government sector is much more skill-intensive than the rest of the economy. Thus, it is difficult to absorb unskilled or disadvantaged workers into state and local government jobs.

Even when there was a legislative mandate to local and state governments to reform their civil service procedures or restructure jobs to help disadvantaged workers obtain public-service employment monies, little happened. Moreover, because the salaries offered under public-service employment programs exceeded by a large margin the average yearly wages of some thirteen million workers, these jobs looked attractive even to those in the labor force who were not remotely considered to be disadvantaged. Managers of state and local government agencies, instructed to hire new workers with the federally provided funds, would therefore have a large pool of

---

[1] "An Impact Evaluation of the Public Employment Program," Technical Analysis Paper no. 17 (Washington, D.C.: U.S. Department of Labor, Office of the Assistant Secretary for Policy Evaluation and Research, Office of Evaluation, April 1974).

more-than-qualified workers. Under pressure to be "good" managers, those in charge of hiring would naturally choose the better-qualified candidates. That is not to say that the public jobs programs were totally ineffective in aiding low-income individuals. Studies have shown that the Neighborhood Youth Corps, Operation Mainstream, and Public Service Careers did indeed transfer income to unskilled workers. However, there was no long-lasting effect. In other words, the income-earning potential of the participants in these programs was not improved substantially.

Whether or not one believes that government jobs programs are effective, the problem of lags must be taken into account. A federal jobs program is presumably instituted as a **counter-cyclical measure.** That means that it must become effective during a recessionary period. Economist Michael L. Wachter of the University of Pennsylvania does not believe that it can be an effective countercyclical tool. "Because of the lags in passage by Congress in implementation, [public jobs program] expansions turn out to be pro-cyclical rather than counter-cyclical." As an example, consider that during the Carter administration expanded CETA enrollments occurred just at the time when the nation was close to full employment. According to Wachter, there is too much uncertainty in economic forecasting and too long a wait before Congress reacts for the federal government to use a jobs program to counter recessions.

An alternative to a public jobs program has been suggested, involving the use of **job vouchers**—a form of subsidized employment. The federal government would send unemployed individuals job vouchers, which they could take to the employer of their choice. The employer who collected the voucher would be reimbursed by the government, and the reimbursement could then be used to pay the worker's salary. In effect, the worker would "hire" the employer, and they would mutually design the tasks to be undertaken by the employee. Such an alternative to public-service employment would appeal to those like Ezra Solomon, a former member of the Council of Economic Advisers, who believe "We already have an awful lot of public employment in this country. I'm not sure the outcry for more is as great as some assume."

Summary

Since the Great Depression, federally provided funds for direct job creation have been used whenever unemployment has seemed excessive. Those in favor of job creation programs believe that labor markets are segmented such that unskilled workers find themselves permanently unemployed. Publicly created jobs therefore will not affect wages and will indeed create employment. Critics of public job creation programs do not believe that labor markets are segmented. To some extent they believe that there will be simply a trade-off of private sector employment for public sector employment. Also, there is a problem of the displacement effect in which federal funds are substituted for state and local funds that would have been used anyway. In any event, the dollars used to provide public jobs have to come from somewhere. To the extent they reduce expenditures elsewhere, they lead to a reduction in employment elsewhere. Therefore, the net effect of direct public job creation may not be very great.

Discussion Questions

1. How does the public jobs program affect the government budget?

2. What is the difference between a tax cut and an increase in public jobs paid for by the fedeal government?

The New Federalism and Automatic Stabilizers

Key Terms

automatic stabilizers Government taxing and transfer programs that change in response to changes in overall business activity; they do not require congressional legislation and tend to mitigate changes in aggregate demand throughout the business cycle.

discretionary fiscal policy Fiscal policy that involves changes in the rate of government spending or in taxes that are exclusively legislated by Congress.

government budget constraint The government's resource constraint. Government spending cannot exceed total financing from taxes, the sale of U.S. Treasury bonds, or money creation.

aggregate demand The sum total of all demand in the economy over a specific time period.

The new federalism was announced as a plan to give back to the states their rightful ability to decide for themselves. Translated into plain English, the plan makes states pay for their own welfare systems. Federalism in principle involves two governmental systems working concurrently—state governments and the federal government. The new federalism presumably gives back to the states more power to decide how government revenues should be spent. Apart from the fact that virtually every state governor rejected the new federalism as a ploy to cut federal government expenditures on needed programs, economists complain that the new federalism would remove the needed impact of **automatic stabilizers** on our on-again, off-again economy. To understand this argument, one must first understand the theory behind such stabilizers.

Automatic stabilizers have to do with fiscal policy, but not the type that is direct or totally discretionary. **Discretionary fiscal policy** involves the federal government either explicitly changing the rate of government spending or explicitly changing taxes. Automatic, or built-in, stabilizers do not require new legislation on the part of Congress. Neither Congress nor the president has to put such built-in stabilizers into motion. The main built-in stabilizers that we have in our economy are the progressive individual and corporate income tax system an unemployment compensation.

Consider the progressive individual income tax. As taxable income goes up, the marginal tax rate also goes up. As taxable income decreases, the marginal tax rate goes down. Think about this for the entire economy. If the nation is at full employment, personal income taxes may yield the government, say, $400 billion per year. Now suppose that business activity suddenly starts to slow down. When this happens, workers are not allowed to put in as much overtime as before. Some workers are laid off and some must change to jobs that pay less. What happens to taxes when wages and salaries go down? Taxes are still paid, but at a lower rate than before since the tax schedule is progressive. People's decreased income puts them into lower tax brackets. The average amount the government takes out of every dollar earned will thereby fall. As a result of these decreased taxes, disposable income does not fall by the same percentage as before-tax income. The individual, in other words, does not feel the pinch of recession as much as we might think if we ignored the progressive nature of our tax schedule.

Conversely, when the economy suddenly comes into a boom period, people's incomes tend to rise. They can work more overtime and can change to higher-paying jobs. However, their disposable income does not go up as rapidly as their total income, because their average tax rates are rising at the same time. Uncle Sam ends up taking a bigger bite. In this way, the progressive income tax system tends to stabilize any abrupt changes in economic activity. (Actually, the progressive tax structure simply magnifies any stabilization effect that might exist.) The corporate income tax is progressive also. The same analysis applied to the individual can be applied to the corporation.

Unemployment compensation is considered an automatic stabilizer also. Throughout the business cycle, it slows down changes in people's disposable income. When business activity drops, most laid-off workers automatically become eligible for unemployment compensation from their state governments. Their disposable income therefore remains positive, although certainly it is less than when they were working. During boom periods, there is less unemployment and consequently fewer unemployment payments made to the labor force. Less purchasing power is being added to the economy because fewer unemployment checks are paid out.

Many students of unemployment compensation benefits point out that these payments truly are a cushion against downturns in the business cycle. Individuals who lose their jobs during recessions and who receive unemployment benefits spend virtually 100 percent of their income. Presumably because of this high propensity to spend, such programs offer a stimulus to the economy during the recession.

By the time the new federalism had started to be discussed in 1982 and 1983, Congress had already acted to end the national trigger on extended benefits from unemployment compensation. Critics of the new federalism believe that the automatic stabilizer of unemployment compensation has already been eroded enough. Shifting the responsibility for key stabilizer programs from Washington to the state and local levels will erode the effectiveness of remaining automatic stabilizers even more. These stabilizers include job training programs, food stamp payments, welfare payments, and so on. The critics contend that the federal government is shifting the spending safety net from where it can provide automatic stabilizers to a sector—state and local governments—that cannot. One must remember that legislation prevents many states from running a budget deficit. Furthermore, cities usually have no taxing authority or they have tax limitations that preclude new tax revenues.

The end result is, presumably, to make the economy more recession-prone and also to increase the severity of future recessions. Not everyone agrees with this analysis, however. Critics of the whole concept of automatic stabilizers point out that the federal government always faces a **government budget constraint.** Therefore, simply because taxes fall during a recession does not necessarily mean that there is any change in **aggregate demand.** After all, if government spending remains the same when taxes fall, the government will run a larger deficit. That deficit must be financed somehow. If it is financed by selling bonds to the private sector, then some expenditures in the private sector will be reduced in order to buy those bonds. For example, fewer private investment expenditures will be undertaken if the federal government succeeds in selling more bonds. In other words, critics of automatic stabilizers maintain that during a recession any increase in aggregate demand due to lower taxes is offset by a reduction in aggregate demand due to the increased sale of U.S. government bonds to finance the increased deficit.

Summary

The new federalism involves giving back to the states the power to tax and spend for numerous welfare programs. Critics of the new federalism maintain that numerous automatic stabilizers will be removed from the economy, thereby exacerbating fluctuations in the rate of growth of the economy. Automatic stabilizers involve progressive corporate and individual income tax systems as well as unemployment benefits, food stamps, and welfare payments. Presumably automatic stabilizers reduce changes in spendable income during the different phases of the business cycle. Critics of automatic stabilizers contend, though, that since the government faces a budget constraint, automatic stabilizers do not, in fact, alter aggregate demand throughout the business cycle but simply involve a trade-off. In other words, if government spending remains the same and taxes fall during recessions, the government must sell more bonds, thereby reducing demand elsewhere.

Discussion Questions

1. How does the progressive corporate income tax act as an automatic stabilizer?

2. What does it mean to say that the government faces a budget constraint? Is this budget constraint similar to the one that you face personally?

Putting a Lid on the Public Debt

Key Terms

gross public debt The total value of all outstanding federal government securities held by agencies of the federal government, individuals, foreign investors, banks, local and state governments, corporations, and insurance companies.

net public debt Gross public debt minus all U.S. government interagency borrowings.

real net public debt The net public debt corrected for price level changes.

crowding-out effect The tendency of deficit-financed government spending to cause interest rates to rise and thereby crowd out private investment or private-planned consumption.

An increase in the federal deficit may be caused by increased government spending on, say, public service employment, without a concomitant increase in taxes collected. Or it may be caused by a reduction in taxes collected because of tax cuts, rebates, or an investment tax credit without a concomitant reduction in government spending. Whatever its cause, any increased deficit in the federal government budget in one way or another leads to an increase in the public debt. Every year for many years now, Congress has debated whether or not it is advisable to increase the "permanent" ceiling on the public debt; after releasing a sufficient amount of hot air, Congress legislates an increase. At one point in the debate, the secretary of the treasury even asked Congress to abolish the so-called permanent ceiling on the public debt.

Why does the size of the public debt matter? Before we can answer that question, we must, in fact, get some idea of that size. The **gross public debt** seems immense—somewhere around $1.3 trillion. But, looked at in other ways, it does not appear so large. First, it is probably best to look at **net public debt,** or gross public debt minus all U.S. government interagency borrowings. After all, what the government owes to itself doesn't have much effect on us. If the Social Security Administration buys a U.S. Treasury bond of $1 million, that $1 million is added to the gross public debt. But this transaction adds nothing to the net public debt. In any one year, interagency borrowing, or debt held by the federal government, is equal to over thirty percent of the gross public debt. Second, we should obviously correct for price-level changes if we want to get an idea of what the **real net public debt** is in terms of current purchasing power. And, third, we should correct for an increase in the population. It is one thing to have, say, a $500-billion public debt when there are only 50 million people living in this country and quite another thing when there are more than 216 million.

If we make these corrections, we find that, until recently, the price-corrected, per capita public debt has been falling. It was lower at the beginning of this decade than it was at the end of World War II. But that is no longer the case. Per capita real net public debt is on the rise, and that means only one thing to Americans—*higher taxes in the future.*

Here we come to a major issue in the debate over how large the public debt should be. When bonds are sold by the United States government (the Treasury), the government has incurred a liability of future payments of interest on that debt and, eventually, repayment of the principal. Ignoring for the moment the repayment of the principal (we can assume that the debt is constantly refinanced when it comes due), any increase in the public debt means an increase in future interest payments. All other things held constant, this means that taxpayers in the future will have to pay more taxes to meet these increased interest payments. There is a popular saying in economics that there is no such thing as a free lunch, and this saying applies to government spending also.

With full employment and a stationary economy, whenever the government spends more than it receives, someone else has to reduce spending to release resources so the government can carry out that extra spending. In other words, at any given time the pie is only so large. The private sector must give up what the government takes. Thus, to find out how much the government takes out of the private sector, we do not look at *explicit* taxes collected in any one year; we look at the total amount of government spending because that spending must be paid for in one way or another. When debt is issued to pay for it, some parts of the private sector voluntarily give up spending that they would otherwise plan in exchange for the government's promise to pay interest on a bond and eventually repay the principal. In later years, other sectors in the economy—that is, taxpayers in general—not so voluntarily give up some of their spending capacity in the form of higher taxes (or higher inflation!) to pay the interest on bonds already issued. In any event, public debt domestically purchased is a debt that we owe ourselves.

In this sense, there is little difference between taxation and debt financing of government spending. In the extreme case, there is no difference at all if taxpayers are not fooled, even temporarily. They know that, when the government runs a deficit and issues more debt, they will be forced to cough up more tax dollars in the future to pay for those interest payments on that increased debt. When taxpayers have perfect foresight, they alter their behavior accordingly by saving more when there are large increases in the government deficit than they would otherwise. This increased saving by taxpayers yields them interest with which to pay future higher taxes levied to pay interest on government debt.

Even if taxpayers don't catch on immediately, they might catch on if the federal government went into large deficits year in and year out. In any event, the private loanable-funds markets (or capital markets, as they are somtimes called) have long been aware of the effects of increased deficits. The federal government cannot ask the capital markets to cough up some $100 billion in a one-year period—as it did between 1982 and 1983—without producing an effect. In fact, with a given amount of credit available, the only way the government could do this is by sweetening the deal, or offering higher interest rates. But these higher interest rates lead to the **crowding-out effect.** As a result, the public sector expands and the private sector contracts, but with little effect on the growth rate of aggregate demand. So from two points of view, increases in the public debt brought about by increased federal government deficits can be treated as having the same effect as an increase in current taxes.

If this is the case, there is not much to be said in favor of the argument that increasing the public debt imposes a burden on future generations in the sense that they will be enjoying less consumption than would have been possible had the public debt been smaller. Implicit in such a statement is a comparison between increasing the public debt and increasing taxes to pay for current government spending that benefits current generations. But if increasing the debt and raising taxes are analytically the same, then future generations will be in exactly the same place, no matter which form of government finance is used.

Placing a burden on future generations means making them worse off. How are they made worse off? By having a lower real standard of living than they would have had otherwise.

They could have a lower real standard of living only if they inherited a smaller capital stock from the current generation. This would occur if deficit spending, leading to a larger public debt, caused Americans in the aggregate to consume a larger percentage of total income than they would otherwise. Because they would then be saving less, there would be less investment, and the capital stock in the future, which is a function of past investment behavior, would be smaller. But such a scenario will not take place as long as taxpayers realize that increases in the public debt merely mean higher taxes in the future. If they realize this they may save more today in anticipation of higher taxes in the future. Thus, even though the government consumes more, the private sector reduces consumption by a like amount; that is, it increases saving to pay for that higher government spending. In the aggregate, both the rates of consumption and saving stay the same. All that changes is the private-pubic mix of output. Assuming equal productivity in both sectors, future generations will inherit the same capital stock, no matter which form of government finance is used—taxation or increases in the public debt.

Such a scenario is certainly not a foregone conclusion. For example, if taxpayers do not have perfect information about future tax liability, they may be misled into thinking they are better off than they really are when the government spends more and pays for that additional spending by increasing the public debt. Since taxpayers do think they are better off, they may consume more, causing the rate of saving in the economy and also the rate of investment to fall. Future generations will inherit a lower capital stock and will, therefore, be worse off. They will indeed suffer the burden of the public debt.

Summary

In order to get an accurate picture of the size of the public debt, we must calculate the per capita real net public debt.

That figure, until a few years ago, had been declining since World War II. Whenever the per capita real net public debt is rising, Americans can anticipate, on average, higher taxes in the future. Deficit spending leading to a higher real net public debt may simply cause a crowding out of private investment and consumption-planned expenditures. Future generations will suffer from the burden of the public debt if increasing the public debt leads to a lower rate of growth in the future due to lower saving today. Consumption will be higher and saving will be lower today as long as households do not reasonably predict the future result of less saving today in the form of lower real standards of living tomorrow.

Discussion Questions

1. A local school district wanted to increase spending on the school system and asked voters to pass legislation to sell local bonds. Signs around the city stated that "bonds are cheaper than taxes." Are they?

2. Do business firms constantly stay in debt, as does the federal government?

17

The Deficit, Off-Budget Items, and Credit Markets

Key Term

off-budget agencies Those agencies that the federal government owns and controls but whose lending activities do not show up on the official federal budget.

One of the major complaints about large federal deficits concerns their impact on credit markets. The argument goes as follows: The larger the federal deficit, the more available savings (credit) is taken up by the federal government. That means less available savings (credit) to finance state and local government borrowing and private investment. Not surprisingly, the argument continues with its concern over high interest rates. The more the federal government borrows, the higher the interest rates will be.

The numbers that are presented are in terms of "the deficit." The true impact of the federal government deficit on credit markets cannot be seen, however, simply by looking at the size of the officially presented federal deficit. The government uses an accounting procedure that keeps numerous expenditures "off budget." The federal government has additional influence in credit markets due to (1) activities of **off-budget agencies;**

(2) operations of government-sponsored enterprises; and, (3) provision of federally guaranteed loans.

It is crucial to understand that none of these three major loan activities shows up directly in the federal budget. Congress does not vote on appropriations and expenditures involved in these activities. This particular point relates most importantly to off-budget agencies. Their deficits are, for the most part, financed by loans from the U.S. Treasury. The operations of one of these agencies—the Federal Financing Bank—can have surprising effects on the federal budget.

1. *Off-budget Agencies.* The first major type of federal loan activity is the so-called off-budget agencies. All off-budget entities are owned and controlled by the federal government. Examples of off-budget agencies include the Federal Financing Bank mentioned above, the Pension Benefit Guaranty Program, and the Rural Electrification and Telephone Revolving Fund. By law, however, their transactions are excluded from the federal budget. The concerned citizen will not find the appropriations for these agencies included in the budget totals, nor will he or she find the outlays of these off-budget agencies subject to ceilings set by congressional budget resolutions. Off-budget borrowing has grown significantly, from $1 billion in fiscal year 1974 to $31 billion in fiscal 1983.

The most important of these off-budget agencies is the Federal Financing Bank (FFB), which began operation in 1974. Today it provides most of the financing for off-budget agencies and also for certain on-budget agencies. The FFB lends by three methods: (1) purchasing agency debt, (2) purchasing loans and loan assets, and (3) purchasing loan guarantees. All of these purchases are made by borrowing directly from the Treasury. It should be understood that the original purpose of the FFB was simply to coordinate the borrowing of a number of federal agencies. It was designed simply to act as an intermediary— buying securities those agencies issued and paying for them with funds borrowed from the Treasury. As designed, then, funds lent by the FFB to off-budget agencies would not show up in the budget totals which Congress votes on and authorizes.

Federal agencies often guarantee loans to insure the lender against any loss as a result of default by the borrower. Some of the most famous cases of loan guarantees involved New York City, Chrysler, and Lockheed. When the FFB purchases a guaranteed loan, for example, at the request of a federal agency, that purchase is ultimately paid for by the Treasury, which will probably sell U.S. government securities to cover the expense.

In effect, such an action is a direct loan from the Treasury to the private sector borrower, but it's a "loan" that will not show up anywhere in the federal budget or deficit. Nonetheless, total borrowing by the Treasury will be higher to finance the purchase. The crucial point to understand is that Congress has no direct control over these increases in federal spending financed by FFB purchases of guaranteed loans.

2. *Government Sponsored Enterprises.* The second major federal involvement with credit markets consists of government-sponsored enterprises which were originally established to perform specific credit functions but are now privately owned. Although the transactions of these enterprises are not included in the federal budget, they are subject to government supervision. Three of these agencies operate under the watch of the Farm Credit Administration: Banks for Cooperatives, Federal Intermediate Credit Banks, and Federal Land Banks. Three agencies support the housing market: The Federal National Mortgage Association (Fannie Mae), the Federal Home Loan Banks, and the Federal Home Loan Mortgage Corporation (Freddie Mac).

3. *Guaranteed Loans or Mortgage Pools.* The third category consists of the so-called federally guaranteed mortgage pools or loans for which the federal government wholly or partly insures or guarantees payment of the loan principal and/or interest. Like the off-budget agencies and federally sponsored agencies, federal loan guarantees do not show up in the federal budget. The bulk of loan guarantees have been used to support housing; however, in recent years, guarantees have been used increasingly for other purposes, for example, the loan guarantees involving New York City and Chrysler.

The fact is that today more than three-fourths of federal lending occurs outside the federal budget. This federal lending is not subject to review by Congress. In 1982, for example, on-budget direct loans were $28.1 billion, off-budget direct loans were $26.2 billion, and guaranteed loans were $101.8 billion. Of outstanding federal loans in that same year, on-budget loans were $101.7 billion, off-budget loans were $114 billion, and guaranteed loans were $408 billion. A political question comes with a program of such size: Why has there been such little criticism of how federal credit programs are expanding without congressional approval? Perhaps the answer to the proliferation of the 358 different federal credit programs lies in the politics of government spending. Critics of such programs argue that Congress and the executive branch have discovered that by keeping the majority of such loan activity off the budget, they can provide help to constituents without appearing to be extravagant to the general public.

Summary

The impact of the federal government on credit markets cannot be measured simply by looking at the reported deficit. Numerous federal credit activities take place every year without being part of the official federal government. Direct loans are made that are not considered part of the budget. Numerous federally guaranteed loans are also made. In fact, three-fourths of all federal credit activities do not show up on the budget. Politically, it may be easier for politicians to provide benefits to individuals and special-interest groups via off-budget credit activities, because taxpayers do not directly see the cost to them and to society.

Discussion Questions

1. Would an accounting procedure change, in which all off-budget activities were shifted to on-budget, alter the true cost of the federal government to the American public?

2. Since a federal loan guarantee does not directly appear to be a cost to taxpayers, how indeed can such guarantees impose a cost on taxpayers?

3. Why do businesses prefer federally guaranteed loans to normal loans when they need to borrow money?

The Full Employment Budget Rides Again

Key Terms

full employment budget The size of the federal government budget if the economy were operating at full employment.

full employment deficit The size of the federal government deficit if the economy were operating at full employment.

full employment surplus The size of the federal government's surplus if the economy were operating at full employment.

potential real GNP Potential real output, or the level of real GNP that the economy could produce if all resources were fully employed.

Back in 1962, President Kennedy and his advisers were pushing tax cuts. They didn't have supply-side economists to help them out, so they resorted to something called the **full employment budget** concept. The full, or high, employment budget is defined as what the federal government budget would be if the economy were operating at full employment. In other words, one can talk about a **full employment deficit** or a **full employment surplus** position. These deficits or surpluses may vary dramatically from actual deficits or surpluses. President Kennedy's Economic Report offered the logic that if his tax cut were enacted, the full employment government budget would not be in deficit (even though the actual one would be). In 1973 the President's Economic Report again noted that the full employment budget was the only budget to look at for policy considerations. Indeed, it was hailed as the "best single guide to budget policy" since it presumably represented the desired rate of growth of the nation.

There is some truth to the fact that looking at the actual deficit or surplus (the latter being more rare) may not give a true indication of what is actually happening. Consider the following situation: Suppose the economy is at full employment and the government budget is in balance. Then the economy goes into a recession and incomes fall. The government, however, does nothing. Government spending remains the same. But since some taxes are based on income, government revenues fall also. A formerly balanced budget goes into deficit. This budget deficit should certainly not be regarded as an active stimulating policy decision on the part of the government. It is merely a result of the recession, not a counterrecessionary move. Otherwise stated, if you don't know at what percentage of its potential the economy is operating, you can't really tell how active fiscal policy has been merely by looking at deficits and surpluses.

In order to estimate the full employment budget, one needs to estimate **potential real GNP,** or the level of real gross national product at which the economy would be operating if all resources were fully utilized. The government estimates potential real GNP (corrected for inflation) by looking at (1) the working age population, (2) the ratio of the labor force to total population, (3) the ratio of total employment to total labor force, and (4) the ratio of real GNP to employment. One of the major estimates involved in figuring full employment, or potential real GNP, is the difference between actual unemployment and the rate of unemployment that would occur at full employment. In 1955 this so-called full employment rate of unemployment was estimated at 4 percent. In 1971 it was estimated at 5.1 percent, and today it is estimated at about 6 percent. The increase in the full employment rate of unemployment is due to an increase in the number of younger persons in the labor force who exhibit a higher-than-average unemployment rate.

Once potential real GNP has been estimated, government analysts attempt to measure the full employment amount of tax revenues that would be collected if the economy were at full employment. So analysts have to have some estimate of how tax receipts would increase if different types of income were increased to their full employment level. For example, it is estimated that the individual income tax goes up by about 1.4 percent for every 1-percent increase in GNP. The figure is somewhat less for corporate income taxes—about .8 percent. That is to say, a 1-percent increase in GNP leads to a .8-percent increase in corporate taxes collected.

Of course, tax revenues are only one side of the government accounting coin. The other side involves expenditures. Here analysts must estimate the relationship between changes in employment and changes in government expenditures. Most government expenditures are insensitive to cyclical fluctuations in employment and GNP. In other words, the majority of actual expenditures are the same at full employment or less than full employment. Several automatic stabilizers are not, however. For example, unemployment benefits are sensitive to changes in employment. So, too, are Social Security benefits and food stamps. The estimate is that a decrease in one percentage point in the unemployment rate results in a decrease of $3.3 billion in these types of expenditures.

Has there been much difference between the actual budget deficit and surplus and the high employment deficit and surplus? Yes, substantial differences have existed. In 1976, for example, the actual budget deficit was $56 billion, but the full employment budget deficit was only about $20 billion. In 1978, the actual budget showed a deficit of $27.7 billion, but the full employment deficit was $13.4 billion. In 1979, the actual deficit was $11.4 billion, but the full employment budget was in *surplus* at $5.4 billion. Consider the change from 1978 to 1979. The actual budget seemed to show continued fiscal stimulation. The full employment budget, however, showed a change from expansionary to slightly restrictive fiscal policy.

Critics of the full employment budget approach to an analysis of fiscal policy contend that inflation has not adequately been taken into account. Full employment budget estimates have assumed uniformly that there is no price gap corresponding to the GNP gap and the unemployment gap. In the 1970s and the early 1980s, such an assumption has proven to be unrealistic. Moreover, because of the progressive individual income tax, inflation has increased budget receipts automatically as income has risen with prices: Bracket creep or taxflation has occurred. Budget expenditures have tended to lag, on the other hand, with respect to rising prices. The full employment budget has, therefore, had an inherent bias towards restrictiveness.

Nonetheless, an increasing number of government policy makers are starting to use the full employment budget again as a measure of the basic stance of fiscal policy. The full employment budget still allows the analyst to separate changes in budget conditions that are simply due to changes in economic activity from those that are due strictly to policy changes. Additionally, as the rate of inflation continues to fall in the 1980s, the major criticism of the full employment budget estimation procedure will wither away.

Summary

Mere recitation of actual federal budget deficits and surpluses may not tell exactly what is happening from a policy point of view. A recession leads to reduction in tax receipts. If government spending remains the same, the deficit will increase. This increased deficit, however, cannot be deemed expansionary because it is simply the result of lower overall economic activity. The full employment budget attempts to solve this problem by giving an estimate of what the deficit or budget would be if the economy were operating at full employment. A measure of potential real GNP must be obtained. Once this measure is obtained, then the difference between the actual situation and what would prevail if potential real GNP were attained is calculated. This calculation is applied to federal government tax receipts as well as federal government expenditures. The resulting deficit or surplus is called the full employment deficit or surplus. Some critics claim such a figure is meaningless in a period of high inflation.

Discussion Questions

1. Does the fact that the federal government is running a full employment surplus when it is running an actual deficit change the deficit's impact on private citizens?

2. Why is the notion of the full employment budget used more frequently when presidents want tax cuts?

PART FOUR

Inflation

What the CPI Really Means

Key Term

market basket of goods A representative combination of goods and services that the average consumer presumably purchases.

It has not been uncommon in recent years to read that the cost of living rose last year by 5, 6.2, or 10 percent. Nor is it uncommon to learn that the cost of living rose last month at a projected annual rate of, say, 12 percent. However, there is no such thing as a cost-of-living index, at least not of the kind we normally think of as an index. The Department of Labor Bureau of Labor Statistics (BLS) compiles price indices and issues changes in them monthly. However, the BLS is quick to point out that changes in what is called the consumer price index (CPI), do not represent changes in any cost-of-living index. That name is misleading and is not, according to the BLS, a reliable gauge of current living costs.

Well, if it's not a gauge of current living costs, what is it? It is a measure of the change in prices of a **market basket of goods** and services purchased by a typical urban worker's family in 1972 and 1973. At that time, the BLS made a survey

105

of the proportions of a typical worker's expenditures that went for medical costs, housing, clothes, and so on.

Right away we can see a bias in the measure of changes in the CPI because expenditure patterns may have changed since 1973. Individuals respond to changing tastes and changing relative prices. As the relative price of certain goods increases, the proportion spent on those goods generally decreases (other things held constant). For example, both increased concern about animal fats and the higher relative prices of meat have reduced beef consumption markedly. Nonetheless, the CPI continues to assume that consumers spend fifteen percent of their food budget on veal and beef. Thus the CPI will overstate any price increase for part of the market basket of goods and services because, in actuality, consumers will not be buying as much of that good or service as before, when its relative price was lower. On this score, the CPI is biased upward.

Moreover, many things that were bought in the early 1970s are not bought any more, and things that were not available then and, therefore, were not included in the market basket of goods are now available and being bought. Here again, we detect a bias in the measurement of the CPI.

The CPI appears to be particularly biased upward in its assessment of the cost of owning a home. For example, in the first quarter of 1979, the Bureau of Labor Statistics estimated that the cost of owning a home rose at a 12.6-percent annual rate. Another government agency, the Department of Commerce's Bureau of Economic Analysis, estimated that the cost of home ownership rose at only a 5.5-percent annual rate during that same time period. The CPI overestimate comes from the fact that the BLS assumes that a certain proportion of the population buys and finances a home every year. In recent years, there have been dramatic increases in mortgage interest rates and housing prices. The cost of a house, however, is amortized over a twenty- to thirty-year period, the usual length of a mortgage. Nonetheless, the CPI treats real estate the same as it treats an apple: The full price of both purchases is figured into the index. Also consider the fact that housing is partially consumption and partially investment. The benefits from the appreciation in real estate are not figured into the CPI, but all the increased costs of home ownership, such as higher real estate taxes, are. In 1981, 1982, and 1983, consumers purchased a number of homes using "creative" financing. Creative financing basically involves the seller of the home becoming a partial mortgage banker. Implicitly, so-called creative financing basically meant a reduction in the sale price of new and used homes during that period. Within the next several years, the BLS is going to change the way in which it computes the housing part of the CPI; that way, there may be less bias in the index the next time there are abrupt changes in housing prices and/or mortgage interest rates.

An additional bias in the CPI involves its inability to take account of changes in the quality of goods and services. Generally, higher-quality items cost more. For example, one reason medical care is more expensive is because it is of higher quality than in the past. Thus, its price per constant-quality unit has certainly not gone up as much as its nominal price. However, as the CPI is measured, few changes in quality are taken into account. One researcher, Robert J. Gordon of Northwestern University, tried to take account of quality changes for the equipment that manufacturers use in producing their output. He looked at such quality changes as increased energy efficiency and increased machine output per dollar of capital cost. For the period 1947 to 1979, the index Gordon constructed rose only about one-tenth as much as the index constructed by the Commerce Department's Bureau of Economic Analysis!

The evidence shows, on net, that the CPI overstates the rate of inflation. There is serious opposition, however, to altering the methods used in constructing the CPI. For example, the BLS advisory panel argued against changing the way in which the housing component of the CPI is calculated. There was also particular opposition from organized labor. Why? Because the members of organized labor benefit from a high reported

rate of inflation, either directly through cost-of-living adjustments (discussed in chapter 22) or because the CPI is a major
factor in their wage-demand calculations. Indeed, when a new
CPI was under construction a few years ago, George Meany of
the AFL-CIO and Leonard Woodcock of the United Auto Workers both expressed opposition to constructing an all-inclusive
index that would cover everyone in the economy. The older
index was limited to urban wage earners and clerical workers.
Meany and Woodcock knew that an all-inclusive index would
show a lower rate of inflation. Thus, any cost-of-living clauses
in their union contracts would be less lucrative. A partial solution had to be agreed upon; the BLS started two indexes in
1977—an updated version of the older CPI, which is limited
to urban wage earners and clerical workers, and a broader CPI
for all urban households.

Summary

The Bureau of Labor Statistics is quick to point out that changes
in the consumer price index, or any price index for that matter,
cannot be called changes in the cost of living. Rather, they are
simply changes in an imperfectly measured index of the average
price level. Currently, the CPI suffers from many biases. One
bias involves using an inappropriate market basket of goods
that was chosen in 1972–73 when the relative price of meat,
energy, and housing was lower than it is currently. Since consumers substitute away from relatively more expensive items,
this fault in the CPI causes an upward bias. The CPI also is
unable to take account of changes in the quality of goods and
services.

Discussion Questions

1. In any given month, a very small percentage of American
households purchase a home. This being the case, what is an

appropriate way to include the cost of housing in any price index?

2. What are some of the ways that you could assess your individual situation in terms of the changes in the prices of the goods and services that you use compared to changes in the consumer price index?

Can Consumers Help fight Inflation?

Key Term

circular flow of income and product The flow of goods and services from firms to households and of factors of production from households to firms counterbalanced by the flow of expenditures from households to firms and payments to owners of factors of production from firms to households.

Can the consumer help in the fight against inflation? Yes, say Arthur F. Burns, former chairman of the Federal Reserve Board, and his close associates at the board. About a decade ago, Burns said that America had become a nation of impulse shoppers and gadget buyers and that such behavior was contributing to inflation. Careful budgeting and comparison shopping were the remedies. In an interview with one of Burns's high-ranking associates, the consumer magazine *Changing Times*[1] obtained more specifics on the issue. Could consumers help fight inflation, and, if so, how?

It was admitted that the major responsibility for dampening inflation lies in appropriate government policies. But the con-

---

[1]*Changing Times,* September 1974, pp. 41–43.

sumer can help. How? By shopping more wisely, consumers can alert manufacturers and retailers that they must sell on a price-competitive basis. Consumers must give a loud signal to manufacturers and retailers that, in the future, spending will be guided by prices. Frills and extras will be avoided, and luxury models must be downgraded to utilitarian ones.

The high-ranking economist of the Fed (Federal Reserve Board) agreed with *Changing Times* that, in the past, the American consumer was quite price-conscious. However, as any society becomes more affluent, it becomes "difficult to keep the consumer behaving in a price-competitive way." Now consumers are richer and don't take as much time to stretch their incomes further. This leads to impulse buying, which presumably means that manufacturers and retailers can sell items at higher prices than they would otherwise.

Let's start with a given: Each consumer has a limited amount of resources—time and assets. If the consumer does not increase his or her average checking account balance or amount of cash on hand, then we can say that the consumer either spends or saves all his or her income. Income used for spending is put into the **circular flow of income and product.** Income saved enters the same flow of income and product but in a roundabout manner, by going into savings institutions, to stock market purchases, and so on, and by being used to finance housing and other investments that, in effect, put the savings back into the circular-flow expenditure stream.

At what place in this flow can the consumer, by wiser shopping, reduce the rate of inflation as Burns and his associates suggest? If consumers devote more of their time (which is not a free good) to comparison shopping and, in effect, get the same quantity of goods they were going to buy but with lower money expenditures, they will have more purchasing power left after they have bought everything they had planned to buy. What do they do with this extra purchasing power? If they keep it under their mattresses, then Burns's suggestion might indeed reduce the rate of increase in prices, at least for a short period, because consumers actually would reduce aggregate demand. But what if consumers take this extra purchasing power, reaped from comparison shopping, and decide to save it by putting it in a savings and loan association?[2] That purchasing power will simply be reinjected into the expenditures stream by way of the capital market. The savings and loan association will use the extra savings to purchase more mortgages, thereby allowing more home building. Thus, the growth rate of aggregate demand is not reduced, nor, consequently, is the rate of inflation. It could be argued that eventually this increased amount of saving will lead to a greater capital stock and, therefore, higher productivity for American workers and a lower price level.[3]

This scenario is a possibility but a strange one. Why should American consumers desire to save a larger percentage of their income just because they spend more time comparison shopping to get better deals? It is hard to find such a theory of saving behavior. It is more likely that, if consumers spend more of their time comparison shopping (and, hence, "purchasing" less leisure), they will merely spread their purchasing power over a larger number of items because they are getting a better deal on each one of them. Aggregate demand will not change, nor will there be any change in inflationary forces.

No matter how charitably we assess the analysis by the members of the Fed, their suggestions will not yield a plan that would actually lower the rate of inflation. It is possible, although highly improbable, that getting consumers to shop more wisely could mean a once-and-for-all reduction in the absolute price level. But it is hard to see how it could mean a permanent reduction in the *rate* of inflation—that is, the rate of price rises

---

[2]An increase in checking account balances can be treated similarly by considering commercial banks as financial intermediaries.

[3]But at the cost of inefficient use of consumers' time.

year in and year out. Suppose impulse shopping stopped, comparison shopping became widely popular, and, as a result, a number of manufacturers found that they had to lower their prices to continue to sell the same quantity of goods. The price level, as measured by the Bureau of Labor Statistics, would then either fall or not rise as rapidly one year as it would have otherwise. But how could this change in consumer buying activity permanently affect the rate of rise in prices? Burns and his associates gave no answer to the interviewer from *Changing Times.*

Summary

It has been suggested that one way to fight inflation is to get consumers to stop impulse shopping, to shop more wisely instead, and to engage in comparison shopping. However, comparison shopping involves the use of time, which is a scarce resource. Additionally, given no change in the amount of cash and checking account balances that people hold, and given no change in the proportion of their income they save and can spend, comparison shopping could not possibly lead to a reduction in the rate of growth of aggregate demand and, hence, in the rate of inflation. Comparison shopping simply would lead to lower prices for some items, but then consumers would spend the leftover income on other items causing their prices to rise.

Discussion Questions

1. What incentive does the Federal Reserve Board have to offer a theory of inflation that involves consumers rather than government agencies?

2. What is the difference between a once-and-for-all change in the absolute price level and a change in the rate of inflation?

Attempts at Controlling Prices

Key Terms

cost-push theory of inflation A theory in which inflation is touched off by a spontaneous rise in wages, profit margins, commodity prices, or other elements of cost.

profit-maximizing price The price which generates maximum total profits for the firm. A price below or above will generate lower total profits.

inflationary premium Additional interest creditors demand to take account of anticipated future inflation that will reduce the value of the dollars that the creditors are paid back for loaning money.

market-clearing price The price at which the quantity demanded equals the quantity supplied so that there are no unfulfilled aspirations on the part of either buyers or sellers at that price.

shortage The excess quantity demanded at a particular price which is below the market-clearing price.

black market The market in which goods and services are sold at prices above their legal maximum.

constant-quality units Units of commodities for which quality is held constant; to estimate price per constant-quality unit requires that all units of different qualities first be adjusted for differences in quality.

repressed inflation A situation in which there are underlying expansionary forces occurring that cannot manifest themselves in higher published prices because of effective price controls.

published price The price that the seller of a good or service publicly provides or announces.

transactions price The actual price at which an exchange takes place.

Price controls have been around for a long time. Rome was using them for centuries before the birth of Christ. However, the first recorded extensive price-control program was instituted in A.D. 301 by the Emperor Diocletian. His price-control edicts set schedules for 890 different price categories, more than 200 of which were for food. Anyone caught disobeying the emperor's edict was dealt with severely—death by drowning. According to the historian Lactantius, writing in 1314, there was

> . . . much bloodshed upon very slight and trifling accounts; and the people brought provisions no more to market since they could not get a reasonable price for this; and this increased the dearth so much that after many had died by it, the law itself was laid aside.

Medieval Europe, of course, had its own set of price controls; a "just price" code was firmly established. And the colonies in the New World had price controls. In 1636 the Puritans set up wage and price limitations. Those who violated the code were officially classified with "adulterers and whoremongers."

During the American Revolution, controls were quite popular. The Continental Congress set price ceilings on October 20, 1774. It decreed "that all manufacturers of this country be sold at reasonable prices" and that "vendors of goods or merchandise will not take advantage of the scarcity of goods, . . . but will sell the same at rates we have been respectively accustomed to for twelve months last past." In 1775, the ceiling price on turkeys was nine cents a pound; on milk, nine cents a gallon; and on rum, sixty-three cents a gallon. Lodging at local taverns was set at five cents per night. Barbers were prohibited from charging more than three and a half cents for a shave. But such price controls did not prevent inflation. By November of 1777, commodity prices were 480 percent above their prewar average expressed in terms of paper money, or "continentals." General Washington had great difficulty acquiring army provisions at controlled prices. This intensified the agony of Valley Forge. Partly as a result, the Continental Congress declared in June 1778 that "It hath been found by Experience that Limitations upon the Price of Commodities are not only ineffectual for the Purposes proposed, but are likewise productive of every evil Consequences to the great Detriment of the Public Service and grievous Oppression of Individuals."

Nonetheless, local and state price controls continued. At some town meetings, the names of those who charged higher than controlled prices were announced, and the guilty were condemned in patriotic newspapers. Boston declared that those who violated price ceilings were enemies of their country. By 1780, most controls were largely abandoned.

This nation's most comprehensive attempt at controlling prices occurred during World War II. And, for the first time in the peacetime history of the United States, extensive wage and price controls were instituted in the 1970s by the Nixon administration. They are indeed popular, not only at home but also abroad. Every European country has tried them in one form or another since World War II.

Many arguments are given for wage and price controls. In most cases, proponents of controls rest their case on the assumption that inflation, or rising *absolute* prices, is the result of cost-push forces due to the monopoly power of either unions or businesses or both. The monopoly theory of rising prices is, at its most basic level, quite simple to understand. Unions attempt to obtain for themselves a larger share of national output by negotiating higher wage rates above some reasonable level. Employers, forced to give in to these "unreasonable" wage demands, pass these higher unit labor costs to the consumer as higher prices. Unions see their wage increases eroded by ever-rising prices and then ask for even higher wages in the future. Thus, a vicious wage-price spiral is started. An alternative **cost-push theory of inflation** involves the "greed" of big businesses. Presumably, businesspeople who want to increase their profits raise their prices. Higher prices produce a higher rate of inflation, and labor quickly catches on to the depreciated purchasing power of its paychecks. Laborers, therefore, demand higher nominal wages in the future. Big businesses see their profits falling, and they, in turn, raise prices even more.

In the face of cost-push inflation, a legislated maximum on both prices and wages would presumably stop inflation or at least slow or limit it. However, cost-push theories of inflation, at least in their simplest forms, are not completely accepted by everyone. After all, a theory is supposed to be able to predict. How can the monopoly business theory or the labor union theory of inflation predict *when* inflation will occur? In other words, how do these examples of the cost-push theory of inflation allow us to say in which future year inflation will get worse? The theories say nothing about when labor unions will use their monopoly power to demand higher wages. Nor do the theories say anything about when business will decide to increase their profits by raising prices. In short, how do these theories explain why some periods are inflationary and others are not? Furthermore, both these theories seem to ignore a crucial economic principle: For a business, even a pure monopoly, there is one **profit-maximizing price.** Only if cost conditions or demand conditions change will that profit-maximizing price change. Why then, would monopoly businesses desire to raise prices in some years but not in others? The same is true for labor unions: There is one maximizing wage rate.[1] Once that wage rate is set, an increase in it will be

---

[1]However, there is no general agreement on exactly what unions maximize.

nonmaximizing, unless, of course, demand and/or supply conditions have changed.

Another possible reason to impose wage and price controls involves the notion of expectations. If future inflation is anticipated, economic agents will include this anticipated rate of inflation in all their contracts, both implicit and explicit. Therefore, if the forces that were causing inflation have been reduced, such as through a reduction in monetary and fiscal activity on the part of the government, economic agents may not be aware of the long-run impact of that reduction on the rate of inflation. If wage and price controls can be instituted as a clear signal to economic agents that the inflation is ending, it may alter their anticipations of future inflation and, therefore, reduce the adjustment time to the new, lower rate of inflation.

This scenario appears to be what occurred during the first peacetime price freeze, beginning on August 15, 1971. Nominal long-term interest rates, which include whatever **inflationary premium** the market has decided upon, dropped when the wage-price freeze was instituted. The wage-price freeze had acted as a signal to economic agents that the rate of future inflation would be lower than they anticipated. In spite of wage and price controls, however, the CPI kept rising in 1971, 1972, and 1973. When a second (sixty-day) price freeze was put on in June 1973, long-term interest rates did not fall; they actually rose! From this small bit of evidence, one might argue that wage and price controls can, in fact, break inflationary expectations, but only for a short time, unless the underlying sources of the inflation are reduced or eliminated. If, for example, the inflation is caused by overexpansionary monetary and fiscal policy and nothing is ultimately done to change that policy, no one will be fooled very long by wage and price controls.

Those who have worked intimately with price controls point out that they lead to extreme disruptions in the economy. For example, according to C. Jackson Grayson, Jr., former chairman of the Price Commission, "Wage-price controls lead to distortions in the economic system, which can be minimized only in the short run. No matter how cleverly any group designs a control system, distortions and inequities will appear."[2] Grayson's point rested on some very basic economics. Equilibrium relative prices are determined by supply and demand. When the supply of something becomes relatively more scarce or the demand becomes relatively more intense, the price of the commodity relative to other prices will rise, leading, on the one hand, to an increase in the quantity supplied and, on the other, to a decrease in the quantity demanded. A government-mandated maximum price will not allow such a signaling system to work in the upward direction. To be sure, a maximum price will have no effect whenever the price determined by the forces of supply and demand is below that maximum price. However, when, for whatever reason, the **market-clearing price** exceeds the government-controlled price, a distortion appears. That distortion may take the form of **shortages,** which became painfully evident after the Nixon price-control program lingered on; or it may take the form of **black markets,** which were rampant in this country during World War II; or it may take the form of ingenious systems of evading or avoiding the controls (which activity per se constitutes a loss of social product). In any event, the control has the effect of distorting the flow of resources in the economy. This leads to a lower economic welfare for the nation as a whole.

Moreover, some practical problems are inherent in any price-control system. Attempting to police the controls on millions upon millions of wages and prices is a task of overwhelming magnitude. During World War II, we had approximately 60,000 paid price watchers and something like 300,000 to 350,000 volunteer price watchers. The time and effort devoted to polic-

---

[2]C. Jackson Grayson, Jr., "Controls Are Not the Answer," *Challenge,* November-December 1974, p. 10.

ing wage and price controls use economic resources that are, by definition, not free. Moreover, although it is perhaps possible to control nominal prices, it is literally impossible to control the real price per **constant-quality unit.** In the face of a maximum nominal price, businesses can easily raise the real price per constant-quality unit of the goods they sell merely by lowering the quality. A gallon of gas that now has less octane is more expensive at the same price per gallon in terms of constant-quality units.

The rate of inflation during World War II was lower with price controls than it would have been without them. But what do we mean by the rate of inflation? If we mean the rate of rise in the Consumer Price Index, that may have little to do with the actual rate of inflation. During World War II, the Consumer Price Index rose very little because in most cases any explicit, published rise in prices was illegal! We had then what has been called a **repressed inflation:** An inflation was actually going on, but it did not show up in the official, published price indices. When wage and price controls were lifted after the war, the official price index caught up with the actual price index, and, for two or three years, prices rose at an incredible rate. A basic point can be made here: There is sometimes a difference between a **published price** and a **transactions price.** The transactions price per constant-quality unit of product depends on any legal or quasi-legal arrangements made for the sale of a product, on the quality of the product, on the delivery date of the product, and on the time when the goods must be paid for.

Another question must be asked when price controls are considered in retrospect. What does a price index mean when, during periods of wage and price controls, many goods are in fact no longer available? If I go into the supermarket to buy cans of my favorite soup and they are no longer available, what comfort is it to know that their price hasn't gone up? In fact, the true price of many items during, for example, the 1971–

74 period of controls was actually infinite because they were unavailable. What happens to the true cost of goods when the price of even one item goes to infinity?

During the Carter administration, a system of "voluntary" price controls was introduced. It consisted of numerous guidelines, formulae, and assorted strong-arm techniques that were supposed to keep prices from rising too rapidly. One such technique was the threat of withholding government contracts from firms that granted wage increases in excess of government voluntary guidelines. The courts ruled against the administration's ability to do that because, in effect, such actions would have changed the voluntary system into one that was totally involuntary. Clearly, the Carter administration's attempt at voluntary controls met with little, if any, success. The measured rate of change of the Consumer Price Index was 9.3 percent in 1978 and 11.4 percent in 1979. The rate of inflation slowed dramatically in 1981 and 1982. The threat of mandatory price controls virtually disappeared. You can be certain, however, that if inflation ever takes off again, there will be a public outcry in favor of a new set of wage and price controls. History has a way of repeating itself.

Summary

The history of price controls dates back at least several thousand years. In this country they were used from the very beginning and most extensively during World War II. The arguments in favor of wage and price controls generally involve attempts at curing cost-push inflation caused either by big businesses or strong unions. Additionally, if wage and price controls are instituted along with contractionary monetary and fiscal policies, they may change people's expectations about the future change in prices. Wage and price controls, in any event, lead to disruptions in our market economy because prices are not allowed to clear the market. Shortages and black markets occur. We even see periods of repressed inflation at times of effective wage and price controls.

Discussion Questions

1. How do the concepts of supply and demand relate to the analysis of wage and price controls?

2. What effect does a maximum price have when the market price is less than the maximum legal price?

Resolved:
The U.S. Treasury
Shall Issue
Indexed Bonds

Key Terms

indexation Inserting escalator clauses into contracts, the tax system, etc.

tax bracket An interval of income that is specific and into which a unique and specific tax rate is applied.

escalator, or cost-of-living, clauses Clauses tacked onto contracts that allow for increases in specified nominal values in order to take account of changes in the Consumer Price Index.

real rate of return A rate of return that is corrected for the rate of inflation and is approximately equal to the nominal rate of return minus the rate of inflation.

indexed bond A bond that pays a specified interest rate net of any inflation (real rate of return) each year. Alternatively, a bond whose principle goes up with the rate of inflation.

principal The capital sum that has been borrowed by the issuer of a bond.

Indexation hit the news big in 1981 with the passage of the tax act in that year. Among the many provisions for reforming our tax system was the indexation of federal personal income taxes starting in 1985. Until that time, because the U.S. tax

123

system is progressive with relatively fixed standard deductions and personal exemptions, the federal government will continue to obtain a larger percentage of national income each year without legislating increases in taxes. This phenomenon of bracket creep is well known. Inflation pushes individuals into higher marginal tax brackets even though purchasing power (real income) may not increase. Unless Congress gets cold feet, indexing of the tax system will involve tying personal exemptions and standard deductions to the Consumer Price Index. Tax brackets will be adjusted similarly. The **tax bracket** is a specific interval of income to which a specific and unique tax rate applies. For example, for a childless couple in 1982 in the tax bracket between $3,400 and $5,500, the marginal tax rate was twelve percent. With indexation, this tax bracket and all others will increase at the rate of inflation each year. If there is a ten-percent rate of inflation, the tax bracket will become ten-percent larger.

What impact can we expect tax indexing to have on the federal government? Well, we do have some historical evidence from another country quite close by—Canada. Canada indexed its personal income tax system in 1974. The personal exemption and tax brackets are adjusted annually for increases in the Canadian CPI. During the period 1974–81, indexation coupled with targeted tax reductions resulted in a sharp slowdown of the tax revenues collected. In the five years before indexing, real (inflation-corrected) growth and tax revenues averaged 7 percent a year. Since 1974 it has averaged only .8 percent per year.

Canadian government spending has been reduced sharply, but not so sharply as the decline in tax revenues. Real (inflation-corrected) government expenditures have increased by 2.8 percent a year. Though this is down from the 8.6-percent annual rate from 1969 to 1973, it is not down to the .8-percent increase in tax revenues during the same period. The Canadian federal budget has therefore run a sizeable deficit in the last three years, averaging about 3.7 percent of the gross national product. Canada's experience suggests that indexing in the United States might lead to an increase in annual federal deficits—that is, of course, if Congress doesn't change its mind by 1985 and repeal indexing.

Indexing as it applies to wage and salary contracts has been around for a long time. It involves simply adding **escalator, or cost of living, clauses** to all contracts to avoid any differential rate of adjustment to varying rates of inflation. Nominal obligations are tied to some measure of price changes. Students of this subject date such indexing back to the year 1707, when a restriction on the amount of outside income allowed to Cambridge Fellows was essentially indexed to the price level. The limit had been put on 600 years earlier, and, in the intervening six centuries, prices had indeed risen. Alfred Marshall, in 1886, expressed interest in what he called the "tabular standard." Marshall contended that industry's lack of knowledge about the future value of the English pound caused discontinuities. He suggested that the government should publish tables showing "as closely as may be the changes in the purchasing power of gold, and should facilitate contracts for payments to be made in terms of fixed purchasing power."

American economist Irving Fisher also favored the "tabular standard." In 1925 a company that Fisher helped found actually issued a purchasing-power security; the purchaser of the security was guaranteed a specified **real rate of return** irrespective of the future rate of inflation.

Cost-of-living clauses have been tacked on to labor contracts for some time now. During World War I, cost-of-living clauses were adopted by a number of private employers. But after World War I, when prices began to drop, cost-of-living clauses lost their popularity. Workers were willing to have them used when prices were going up but not when they were going down. In the 1930s, the government experimented with a cost-of-living factor as part of the Economy Act of 1933. That act authorized the president to reduce salaries of federal employees according to cost-of-living changes since 1928. The next year, 1934, several large private companies provided for cost-of-living adjustments based on changes reported by the Bureau of Labor Statistics Index of Prices. During World War II, as inflation became a serious problem, at least half of the collective-bargaining agreements in manufacturing had clauses that allowed the contracts to be reopened when wage increases were needed to match price increases. Such clauses were suspended by the Wage Stabilization Program until the end of the war.

After the war, in 1948, in a General Motors agreement with the United Auto Workers, wages were tied to cost-of-living increases. In the same year, a survey conducted by Rutgers University showed that eighty-eight percent of management and seventy-nine percent of unions opposed such an automatic cost-of-living escalator formula.

Such is not the case today, particularly because future reductions in the price level are improbable. Perhaps 13 million workers are covered in one way or another by wage contracts tying their wages, in part, to changes in the Consumer Price Index. The benefits of some 32 million recipients of Social Security are also linked to changes in the Consumer Price Index. Finally, recipients of food stamps are affected by changes in the CPI.

A wage contract that is indexed is easy to understand. Say an individual worker and employer or a union and employer agree upon a real wage increase of four percent per year; if there is no price change and an individual makes $100 a week this year, he or she will make $104 next year. If, however, during the one-year period there is an inflation of, say, five percent, the worker's wages will automatically be increased by five percent over the $104 to maintain the agreed-upon real wage increase of four percent over the previous year. In the absence of an indexing clause, the worker's real wage rate would have fallen because the actual purchasing power of the money paid will be less than the increase stipulated in the contract.

An **indexed bond** can work in a similar fashion. The purchaser of the bond buys it fully indexed. The seller of the bond agrees to pay an interest rate net of any inflation effect of, say, four percent a year. Assume that the bond cost $1,000. The owner of an unindexed $1,000 bond would merely get $40 each year irrespective of the rate of inflation and would get $1,000 at the maturity date of the bond. However, if the **principal** of the bond were indexed, the owner of the bond would still get $40 a year; but at the maturity date of the bond, the principal would be paid back in terms of the purchasing power of $1,000 when the bond was bought. For example, if the price level had increased by 100 percent while the bond was outstanding, when it was due the owner of the bond would receive back a $2,000 payment for the principal.

The issue of indexing U.S. Treasury bonds became important in the last few years because of the historically very high interest rates that the Treasury had to pay during the 1980s to get people to buy its bonds. These high interest costs would prove to be a boon for bond purchasers. Later on interest rates fell in the economy. The person suffering would, of course, be the taxpayer. On the other hand, in prior periods during the latter 1970s, for example, numerous U.S. government bond purchasers bought bonds yielding relatively low rates of interest only to find that dramatic increases in the rate of inflation wiped out effective yields in purchasing power terms.

The argument has therefore been offered that the U.S. Treasury should issue long-term bonds only on a purchasing power basis—that is, fully indexed bonds. Such a purchasing power bond would provide persons of modest wealth a relatively secure way to hedge against whatever future inflation (or deflation) there might be. Such purchasing power bonds are not really a new idea. Many governments around the world issue these bonds right now. A number of Republican and Democratic members of Congress have cosponsored a bill entitled

"Long Term Savings Restoration Act," which would authorize the Treasury to issue eight twenty-year bonds indexed to the rate of inflation as a means of financing up to half the national debt.

Indexing of bonds, wages, and even tax brackets has its critics. In particular, critics of indexing of bonds and wages see it as signaling a surrender to inflation. Other critics believe that complete indexing of the American economy will lead to higher rates of inflation rather than lower rates. After all, they argue, indexing speeds up the wage-price spiral because if all contracts are indexed, inflation anywhere in the economy is translated into an even more rapid inflation by immediately causing all wages and prices to rise. This argument ignores the fact that indexing serves only one purpose—to equalize the degree of adjustment in *all* sectors of the economy for all individuals for whatever inflation rate exists.

We must remember that indexation treats symptoms rather than the causes of inflation. Indexation is not and never will be a substitute for proper monetary and fiscal policies. At best, indexation offers a way to equalize any burden that inflation imposes on a nation. Every sector of the economy will react equally quickly to a change in the rate of inflation, be it upward or downward. Indexation is not inexpensive, however. Economywide indexing requires resources. It takes resources to make every contract indexed. It takes resources to keep recalculating the prices of things and republishing new price lists. Thus, if the choice were to be made between a zero rate of inflation and a constant rate of inflation, even fully indexed, the former probably would be chosen.

Summary

Indexation involves changing all nominal obligations at the rate of inflation. Indexation of the federal tax system should start in 1985. Then personal exemptions and tax brackets will rise at the rate of inflation as measured by changes in the CPI. Indexation of wages and salaries started many years ago. Currently, Social Security recipients, federal pension recipients, and about 13 million union members have their benefits and wages tied to the rate of inflation through cost-of-living clauses. Indexations of bonds would involve either indexing the principal or indexing the interest. Proponents of indexation particularly want to see U.S. Treasury bonds indexed.

Discussion Questions

1. If you have already reached the highest marginal tax bracket will indexing affect you?

2. What are some of the costs of economywide indexation?

The Costs and Benefits of Inflation

Key Terms

cash balances Currency and checking type account balances.

inflationary tax The tax on cash balances due to inflation. Cash balances depreciate at the rate of inflation, and this is the tax.

depository institutions Any institution that is legally able to take deposits, such as commercial banks and savings and loan associations.

capital gain The difference between the purchase price and the resale price of an asset.

historical cost The actual purchase price of a machine or other asset at the time it was acquired.

replacement value The actual price of replacing a machine or other asset at the current price level.

disinflation A slowing down in the rate of inflation.

monetization of the public debt Reducing the real value of the public debt by the process of inflation.

Lenin was quoted as saying that the best way to destroy the capitalist system is to debauch the currency. Keynes agreed, pointing out that a continuing process of inflation allows governments to confiscate an important part of the wealth of their citizens. "There is no subtler, no surer means of overturning the existing basis of society than to debauch the currency. The process engages all the hidden forces of economic law on the side of destruction, and does it in a manner which not one man in a million is able to diagnose elipses."

But, Keynes further pointed out that while the process of inflation impoverishes many, it enriches some. In other words, there are both costs and benefits from inflation.

First the costs. The major costs of inflation involve:

1. inflation's effect on the use of money,

2. inflation's effect on our tax system, and

3. inflation's effect on our system of relative prices.

Consider inflation and money. By money we mean **cash balances,** currency and whatever one has in checking type accounts. All of us maintain some form of cash or checking account balances because of the convenience they provide. All of us therefore lose value whenever there is an inflation. That is, the purchasing power of the cash held in our wallets or in our checking account balances falls at the rate of inflation.

Take a simple example. Assume that you have stashed $100 away in one-dollar bills underneath your mattress. If at the end of one year there has been an increase in the Consumer Price Index of ten percent, then the purchasing power of those hundred one-dollar bills taken together will be only $90. You will have lost value equal to the ten percent times the amount of cash you kept on hand. In essence, then, the value of the cash we keep on hand depreciates at the rate of inflation. The only way we can avoid this type of **inflationary tax,** as it were, on the cash that we hold is by reducing our cash balances. But reducing cash balances (currency and checking account balances) is not an easy matter. We find that it is beneficial to have money in our checking accounts in order to write checks to pay for the things that we want when we want them, rather than trying to purchase everything at the beginning of a pay period so as to minimize the amount of dollars in our checking account balances or in our wallets.

Thus, a cost to society of inflation is that it increases the individual's cost of holding money, or cash balances. For society as a whole, we probably therefore use too little money during periods of inflation. Note, however, that things are changing. Individuals and corporations are more explicitly being paid to hold money in the form of checking type balances. Since 1981, more individuals and businesses are obtaining interest on funds left in checking type accounts. Eventually, full market rates of interest will be paid on all balances left in checking type accounts at all **depository institutions.** When that occurs, we will no longer be able to say that inflation makes holding money costly. At least not for that proportion of the money supply that is in checking type accounts. Approximately twenty percent of the money supply is, though, in the form of currency issued by the Federal Reserve. Currency can be considered zero-interest-bearing U.S. government bonds with an infinite life (a maturity date in eternity). Those noninterest bearing bonds are depreciating in purchasing power at the rate of inflation. One suggestion has been made to cover this problem—pay interest on currency. That seems a bit farfetched and certainly would create a difficult operational problem if instituted.

The second major cost of inflation has to do with our income tax system. In chapter 4 we pointed out that because of the progressive personal income tax, we have suffered from bracket creep or taxflation. Briefly, individuals are pushed into higher and higher marginal tax brackets, due simply to inflation. This causes marginal tax rates to go up, and, therefore, the average "take" of the federal government has increased. The estimate has been that for every 1-percent increase in the rate of inflation, federal personal tax has increased by 1.5 percent. Inflation has also had an effect on capital gains taxation, business taxation, and the taxation of inventories.

Taxes are levied on increases in the capital values of any asset and are collected when the asset is sold. If you buy a painting (or some common stock) for $1,000 and then three years later sell it for $2,000 because all prices of goods have doubled on average, you have not even maintained your wealth in real terms, because you must pay up to twenty percent of that $1,000 **capital gain** in dollar terms to the government as a tax. You end up poorer than when you began. But had there been no inflation, your later sale of that painting at $1,000 would not have imposed any tax on you and you would at least have broken even. Prices in the United States about doubled during the 1972–81 period, constituting an increase in capital gains tax liabilities even though there was no value gain in real terms of existing wealth.

When businesses purchase assets, such as machines and buildings, they are allowed to deduct as a cost only a certain amount of depreciation each year. For example, if a machine costs $1 million and is supposed to last ten years, under the simplest system of depreciation deductions, the firm can deduct $100,000 a year for ten years from its income before it pays federal corporate profits taxes each year.

In a world of inflation, however, the old nominal value (**historical cost**) of a business's assets fails to reflect the replacement value of the asset that is being depreciated. Under current federal income tax laws, the **replacement value** of the asset cannot be properly adjusted upward to reflect more accurately the higher cost in dollar terms of replacing the depreciating equipment. The result is an overstatement in nominal terms of the actual profit (revenues minus total cost) earned by the firm. This overstatement leads to the payment of higher federal corporate taxes.

Firms hold inventories of raw materials, goods in progress, and finished goods. During a period of inflation, the nominal market value of any inventories held will rise at the rate of inflation. Business firms do not, in general, gain any wealth by the fact that they are able to sell inventories at higher prices at the end of an inflationary period than at the beginning, because the firm must pay a higher price to replace its inventory. Higher money receipts for the inventory sold at the end of a period simply enable the firm to avoid a loss of real wealth. Nonetheless, when a firm is required to estimate so-called inventory profits, it will be taxed on the nominal gain in the market value of inventories held over a specified period. In other words, dollar profits are computed as receipts at new prices minus costs at old prices. While this procedure overstates real profits, taxes must nonetheless be paid on these nominal inventory profits.

Firms have responded to this problem by changing their accounting systems from first-in, first-out (FIFO), in which the cost of goods sold are reported as the price of the first item added to its inventory, to last-in, first-out (LIFO), in which the cost of goods sold are reported as the price of the last item added to its inventory. This change in accounting techniques has reduced, but not completely eliminated, taxes being paid on fictitious nominal profits because of inventory revaluations due to inflation.

The final cost of inflation has to do with its effect on our relative price system. Whenever there is a variable or uncertain rate of inflation, at least three phenomena result which are costly to the economy. They are:

1. More resources are devoted to predicting the rate of inflation and to avoiding the effects of inflation. Individuals will attempt to negotiate escalator clauses into their contracts, a procedure that requires time and effort as well as legal and accounting resources. Entire new institutions arise to accommodate markets in a world of variable, uncertain rates of inflation. Witness what has happened in the mortgage market. It seems as if every year a new type of mortgage contract comes into being in order to take account of wildly changing interest rates, which are often a reflection of wildly changing rates of inflation.

Given that individuals and institutions will be relying more and more on escalator, or cost-of-living, clauses in contracts, more resources will be devoted to more accurate measures of price changes. If 50 million people depend on what has happened to the Consumer Price Index over the last few months, then more resources must go into making sure that the Consumer Price Index is as accurate as is possible, given the resource constraint.

2. Financial planning for the future becomes more difficult. Heads of households will have trouble determining when to make major purchases if they cannot count on changes in prices being constant. Moreover, they will have a more difficult time determining what their saving rate should be today, what type of job to take, and so on, if they are uncertain about the rate of inflation in the future.

3. Comparison shopping time increases for infrequently purchased items. Consumers make choices on the basis of relative prices. For frequently purchased items, such as food, even during a period of inflation that is variable and uncertain, consumers have little difficulty in determining the relative prices of those frequently purchased goods. However, whenever a consumer enters the marketplace seeking a less-frequently purchased major item, such as a washing machine, expensive coats, or a car, that consumer is shocked at how high the prices are. He or she cannot believe that the prices encountered accurately reflect the "true" value of the infrequently purchased item. In order to obtain further information about prices, the consumer feels compelled to search longer than would be the case in a world without inflation or one of constant inflation. Ultimately, the consumer will purchase the infrequently purchased time about as often with and without inflation. But that consumer will have spent more resources in time and comparative shopping efforts before the purchase is made because of inflation.

So much for the costs of inflation to the economy. Associated with some of these costs are benefits to particular groups or institutions in our society. Therefore, as inflation wanes, these groups and institutions end up suffering. Consider the United States government. It, more than any other institution, has been a beneficiary of inflation. How is that again? Well, consider taxflation, or bracket creep, and all of the additional taxes gained through taxes on nominal rather than real increases in asset values. Consider taxes on fictitious inventory gains. All of those put together have made for an effective increase in the revenues going to the federal government that have been monumental and unlegislated. The process of **disinflation** means that federal government (and some state governments using progressive income taxes) will no longer reap the benefits of continued bracket creep.

The federal government also has been a winner with respect to its national debt. During periods of unanticipated inflation, creditors lose and debtors gain. During periods of unanticipated inflation interest rates are not high enough to take account of the cheaper dollars paid back by debtors in the future. In other words, during periods of unanticipated inflation, inflationary premiums added on to interest rates are not high enough. Over the periods during which we have had the most inflation in the last several decades, the largest single net debtor has the United States government. Consider the start of this decade. At that point, the net public debt was around $600 billion. The rate of inflation during that year was ten percent. That meant that the purchasing power of the debt was eroded by ten percent. The owners of those bonds would have to buy an additional $60 billion in bonds in order to keep the purchasing power of their assets constant. Otherwise stated, one-tenth of the real public debt at the beginning of this decade was paid off by inflation. Thus, the lower the rate of inflation, the less the public debt is paid off by inflation. (This, by the way, is a process called **monetization of the public debt.**)

A major group of beneficiaries of inflation over the last few years have been Social Security recipients. By a form of doubled indexation, Social Security recipients have been receiving cost-of-living increases that have been greater than the increase in the Consumer Price Index. As inflation slows, Social Security recipients will no longer receive such large increases in real (purchasing power) benefits. Not surprisingly, this group of individuals has been lobbying for a revision in the Consumer Price Index to take account of the supposed higher prices that retired people have to pay for the same standard of living of middle-aged people.

Finally, another group of beneficiaries of inflation over the past twenty years have been owners of so-called hard assets. Hard assets are defined as anything real, such as real estate, gold, silver, diamonds, jewelry, and antiques. All of these real assets have been considered inflation hedges. In other words, during periods of inflation, the price of these real assets has historically at least kept pace with inflation. Not surprisingly, as inflation took off in the 1970s, the demand for inflation hedges took off also. The result was a run up in the price of real estate, gold, silver, diamonds, and the like. A world of disinflation, however, coupled with higher interest rates on monetary instruments such as bonds, money market mutual funds, and certificates of deposits, have led to a tremendous drop in the price of so-called hard assets. Owners of gold, silver, diamonds, and so on have seen the nominal and real value of their wealth fall dramatically since 1980. As long as the public anticipates low or lower rates of inflation in the future, owners of hard assets will find their wealth positions remaining in a depressed state.

Summary

Inflation imposes a tax on noninterest-earning cash balances, for they depreciate in purchasing power terms at the rate of inflation. This leads to too little use of money. Inflation imposes a cost on private citizens because they are pushed into higher tax brackets simply due to inflation. Also individuals and corporations are taxed on increases in the nominal value of assets owned rather than increases in the real value. Businesses additionally are taxed on increases in inventory profits that may be fictitious, and those businesses are not allowed to deduct the depreciation of their machines and equipment that accurately reflects replacement cost of those machines and equipment. Inflation negatively affects our relative price system by requiring individuals to spend more resources protecting themselves and engaging in comparison shopping. The main beneficiary of inflation has been the federal government because of bracket creep and because of the monetization of the public debt. The owners of hard assets have benefited by inflation and are suffering because of disinflation.

Discussion Questions

1. The value of most hard assets has fallen dramatically in the 1980s. Does this mean that hard assets do not have an intrinsic value?

2. Some say that debtors gain and creditors lose when there is inflation. Is this statement strictly correct?

PART FIVE

Banking
and
the
Fed

Should the Fed Be Controlled?

Key Terms

monetary rule A rule by which the Federal Reserve would be required to increase the money supply in circulation at a fixed annual rate, such as five percent per year.

depository institutions' reserves Reserves held either in the form of non-interest-bearing deposits held by district federal reserve banks or in the form of vault cash.

Article 1, Section 8, of the United States Constitution says that Congress shall have the power to "coin money and regulate the value thereof." Some of this power was delegated to the Federal Reserve System when it was created in 1913. The Board of Governors of the Federal Reserve System is an independent agency. If you look in the *Congressional Directory,* the Federal Reserve is listed along with the American National Red Cross and the Appalachian Regional Commission.

Congress apparently intended that the Fed remain independent in order to isolate it from the political pressures that might arise if it were an agency of Congress or of the executive branch. In the past, the chairmen of the Federal Reserve Board of Governors have cherished, and indeed assumed as immutable, the Fed's independent status.[1]

But this has not been so in the last few years. Congress has repeatedly indicated its desire to place controls on the Fed's activities, because Congress has been persuaded by the press, academicians, and others that the Fed does, indeed, control much of the fate of economic activity in the United States.

Critics of the Federal Reserve maintain the following:

1. The Great Depression would not have been "great" if the Federal Reserve had not allowed the money supply to decrease by so much during the period 1929–33.

2. The recession at the beginning of the 1960s would not have occurred had the rate of growth in the money supply not been cut back so sharply.

3. The credit crunch of 1966 could have been avoided if the Fed had not so drastically reduced the rate of growth in the money supply.

4. The rate of inflation and the rate of growth in the money supply (under the Fed's control) were greater in the 1970s than in any other peacetime period in the United States except after World War II, with the latter causing the former.

5. The variability in the rate of growth in the money supply has been greater since the 1960s than at any other time in the peacetime history of the Fed.

Given these complaints, Congress passed resolutions directing the Fed's activities. This had never before occurred in the history of the Federal Reserve System. For example, in 1975 Congress passed a resolution introduced by Senator William

---

[1]Except from 1942 to 1951, when the Fed agreed to keep the interest on government bonds pegged.

Proxmire directing the Fed to take appropriate action in the last half of the year to increase the money supply at a rate substantially higher than in the recent past. This joint congressional resolution requires that the Fed report to Congress every six months to indicate its goals in terms of the growth rate in the money supply. Prior to this resolution, the desires of the Federal Reserve's Open Market Committee were first known ninety days after the meetings took place; this was later changed to forty-five days. In another vein, Congress has proposed that the Fed be subjected to a Government Accounting Office audit on a regular basis. The congressional resolution that requires the Fed to report to Congress may turn out to be one of the most important congressional actions affecting the Fed, and the banking system in general, for a long time. Currently, the chairman of the Board of Governors of the Federal Reserve System must report to the House every six months and also to the Senate every six months, but starting three months later. Thus, every three months, the Fed is required to present to Congress its explicit goals in terms of the growth rate of the money supply and how well it has succeeded in reaching its money-supply growth goals. Some observers contend that such explicit reorting of goals and accomplishments by the Fed to the Congress at regular three-month intervals will prevent the Fed from greatly overshooting or undershooting some "reasonable" long-run growth rate in the money supply, as it has done many times in the past.

There is no question that the atmosphere has changed in Washington. The Fed is no longer a sacred cow; it may, in fact, by the time you read this book, be subjected to even more controls by Capitol Hill. The question of whether or not the Fed should remain independent is really a question about the past and future expected performance of the Fed. Even accepting the criticism that the Fed has, indeed, been responsible for many recessions and inflations does not logically necessitate the solution of making the Fed more answerable to Congress.

Indeed, one might conjecture the opposite: the solution would be to isolate the Fed totally from Congress, the president, and any other political body—in fact, to isolate it totally from the vagaries of any human efforts at manipulating the growth rate in the money supply intended to alter interest rates, the rate of unemployment, the growth rate of capital formation, or what have you. Such independence for the Fed could be achieved by what some call a **monetary rule.** A monetary rule would require that the Fed increase the money supply (defined as currency and checking type account balances) at a specific rate—say, five percent a year. At least in the long run, there is little question that the money supply can be controlled by the Fed through its control over **depository institutions**[1] **reserves.** In fact, researchers at one Federal Reserve Bank (in St. Louis) worked up a simulation model showing exactly how the Fed could control the narrowly defined money supply within a very fine range over any three-month period. If a monetary rule were instituted, it would become impossible for Congress, the president, or the sometimes misguided Open Market Committee to exacerbate any boom or bust condition in the economy.

Not everyone thinks that a monetary rule is the answer to the Fed's problems. Those who oppose it contend that the Fed should "lean against the wind" to cut down on the ups and downs in the business cycle. Furthermore, they contend that the elimination of the discretionary power of the Fed would eliminate a valuable and flexible tool of the policy makers.

Summary

The Federal Reserve System was created by legislation passed in December 1913. As created, the Fed has remained an independent agency that in principle cannot be directed by either the president or Congress. Critics of the Fed's independence claim that it has been responsible for such things as the Great Recession and numerous recessions and credit crunches. Currently the chairman of the Board of Governors of the Fed must report to the alternate bodies of Congress every three months, stating target goals for the rate of growth of the money supply and how well the Fed has stuck to those goals. Some critics contend that the Fed should be required to follow a monetary rule in which the rate of growth of the money supply had to be constant at some fixed rate, such as five percent per year.

Discussion Questions

1. If a monetary rule were adopted, what would this mean for monetary policy?

2. What would happen if the Fed were merged with the Treasury Department?

Deposit Insurance and Bank Risk Taking

Key Terms

insolvency A condition when liabilities are greater than assets.

thrift institutions Savings banks and savings and loan associations as well as credit unions.

asset portfolio The array of different types of assets that an institution or individual owns, such as its stocks, bonds, and real estate.

unsecured loans Loans for which no collateral has been put up.

collateral The "backing" for a loan, that is, the assets that can be taken over by the lending institution if the debtor fails to pay off the loan.

One of the most important events in modern banking history was the establishment of Federal Deposit Insurance Corporation (FDIC) in 1934. All members of the Federal Reserve System must belong to the FDIC. The bulk of nonmember banks have also joined. Presently, the FDIC insures deposits of each individual or firm in each bank of up to $100,000. Insured banks must pay a premium equal to one-twelfth of one percent of their total deposits. Similar deposit insurance is available for depositors in savings and loan associations (the Federal Savings and Loan Insurance Corporation, or FSLIC) and depositors in credit unions (the National Credit Union Association, or NCUA).

Virtually all depositors in insured depository institutions have received almost 100 percent of any funds they have had in the depository institution if it failed. Generally, the FDIC forces the failing depository institution to merge with a sound one. In any event, the virtual certainty of not losing a penny due to a bank failure has certainly prevented any talk of a "run" in the banking system.

In the 1930s during the beginning of the Great Depression, banks started to fail. When one bank failed, depositors would force another to fail, no matter how well it was managed, because they would get cold feet and try to withdraw all their funds. No bank has sufficient cash reserves to pay off all depositors at once. As an increasing number of depositors attempted to withdraw their deposits, an ever-increasing number became **insolvent.** Then there was a "run" on the banking system. In recent years, certainly, the existence of the FDIC and the FSLIC has prevented a run on **thrift institutions—** savings banks and savings and loan associations. Many of them had become insolvent. A large number of these thrift institutions closed their doors or were forced to merge with others.

Consider the case of Greenwich Savings Bank, which was in serious trouble a few years ago. The FDIC arranged a merger with Metropolitan Savings Bank. In order to get the merger to work, the FDIC agreed to pay back Greenwich's $430-million debt to the Federal Reserve System. The FDIC also agreed to cover Greenwich's interest losses through 1986 and to let Greenwich's $100 million of assets go to Metropolitan Savings Bank. The result? Metropolitan Savings Bank became the second largest mutual savings bank in the country through the merger at no cost to itself. All of Greenwich's depositors, even those with uninsured deposits, didn't lose a penny.

Who, then, lost? Well, the FDIC turned out to be in the hole $185 million, sixty percent of which it will recoup through premiums that its members pay. Note that in this real-world example, the FDIC extended deposit insurance beyond the $100,000 legal obligation. The FDIC and the FSLIC are in effect currently declaring to the banking public that *all* bank liabilities are riskless. You as a depositor don't have to worry how much risk the management of the depository institution takes. If bad investments are made by management, and the depository institution is about to go under, the FDIC or FSLIC will come to the rescue.

The gist of this analysis is that as long as the FDIC and the FSLIC stand ready to repay depositors in full, then depositors no longer care how risky the banks **asset portfolio** is. Riskier assets usually offer higher yields. Indeed, the positive relationship between higher yields and risk is well known in financial circles. Bank management will maximize expected profits now by purchasing the riskiest available assets. Such a decision is rational from the bank management's point of view because depositors are completely insured. In other words, banks have a greater incentive to increase risk because of deposit insurance.

One could argue that such a situation is very tenuous. After all, currently the reserve fund that the FDIC has to cover bank failures is only a little more than one percent of total insured deposits. But the FDIC also possesses a $3-billion credit line from the U.S. Treasury. Finally, we can be almost certain that the Federal Reserve and the Treasury would continue to provide almost limitless support to the FDIC if we ever had a series of serious bank failures. The tax-paying public, therefore, has a substantial interest in the FDIC insurance fund's continued large liability exposure.

In order to counter all banks' incentive to become more risky, a whole series of bank regulations have been imposed. For example, insured banks are subject to a large number of restrictions on the type or quality of assets that they own. They cannot own stocks or significant amounts of real estate.

Unsecured loans (those for which no **collateral** has been put up) may not exceed ten percent of the bank's net worth. They are also not allowed to become closely affiliated with firms in nonbanking lines of commerce. Finally, FDIC engages in numerous bank examinations in order to evaluate the riskiness of bank operations.

Summary

Deposit insurance was instituted during the depths of the Great Depression when banks were failing. The major result of deposit insurance has been to prevent any loss in confidence in the banking system and therefore to prevent a run on the banking system. A perhaps unexpected result of deposit insurance and the most recent behavior of the Federal Deposit Insurance Corporation and of the Federal Savings and Loan Insurance Corporation has been to remove any incentive on bank management to reduce the riskiness of the assets that banks purchase. No matter how poorly a depository institution has been managed, the FDIC and its sister organizations will bail out the troubled depository institution.

Discussion Questions

1. Since the reserve fund of the FDIC amounts to only about one percent of total insured deposits, why aren't we likely to see a run on our banking system?

2. Critics of the FDIC believe that federal deposit insurance should be eliminated entirely, thereby strengthening the impact of market forces on bank management risk-taking decisions. If the FDIC were eliminated, how would that affect depositors?

3. Most insurance premiums vary according to the riskiness of the insured. For example, automobile insurance costs more in major cities than in small towns. Should riskier banks pay a higher price for federal deposit insurance than safe banks?

PART SIX

Stabilization Policies

Stagflation

Key Terms

stagflation A period of simultaneous recession and rising prices.

the Phillips curve A graphic representation of the supposed trade-off between the rate of unemployment and the rate of inflation.

reservation wage rate A wage rate below which an unemployed worker will not accept a job.

frictional unemployment That amount of unemployment that is normal in the economy due to imperfect information and the complexities of the labor market.

"Prices are going up and so, too, is the rate of unemployment." This describes a situation that has occurred on and off since 1969 in the United States economy and elsewhere in the world. The condition has been labeled **stagflation** to combine the notions that the economy is stagnating (as evidenced by the high rate of unemployment) at the same time prices are continuing to rise (as evidenced by an increase in the rate of inflation). An era of stagflation also has been called an era of "slumpflation" because the economy is in a slump while it is inflating.

How can we explain such a paradox? Clearly, a standard macroeconomic analysis, which indicates that prices can rise only when the economy has approached full employment, does not work. Just as clearly, the classical notion of a self-regulating system in which unemployment cannot exist because wages adjust to clear the labor market is also an inadequate explanation. And the cost-push market-power explanation of stagflation (and inflation in general) is inconsistent with the wealth-maximizing models we use in most economic analysis. As we pointed out in chapter 21, the labor union and monopoly market-power theories of inflation do not allow us to predict when the rate of inflation will change. Hence, the cost-push market-power theory is no theory at all but, rather, an *ex post, ad hoc* explanation of what has occurred.

Because periods of stagflation had not occurred prior to 1969, the notion of a trade-off between the unemployment rate and the inflation rate became popular in 1958 with the publication of an article by A. W. Phillips. Phillips discovered an empirical correlation between rates of unemployment and increase rates of wages in the United Kingdom. This trade-off between unemployment and the increase rate of wages, or the inflation rate in general, has been dubbed **the Phillips curve** in honor of its purported discoverer. But this relationship has, in fact, been observed by many for generations and perhaps for centuries. That is, for centuries "good times" (times of rising output) have been associated with high or rising prices, and recessions have been associated with low or falling prices. Economic historians have found references to the so-called Phillips curve trade-off in the works of such diverse writers as the British philosopher David Hume (1779) and the American economist Irving Fisher (1926).

In the last few years, there has been concern that the Phillips curve trade-off may have been "worsening": A higher rate of inflation than in the past is now associated with any given rate of unemployment. The explanation for this worsening trade-off is generally not very convincing. It is sometimes stated that the trade-off has become more disagreeable because of the increased structural rigidity in our economic system, or because of the increased market power of either unions or big businesses. But neither of these analyses is necessary to a plausible explanation of the so-called Phillips curve trade-off and the worsening of that trade-off. To understand stagflation better, we need realize only that information is not perfect in the labor market and that the number of new entrants has been extremely large in recent years. Once we understand that, we can come up with a theory that explains, at least partly, why we observe rising prices and rising rates of unemployment at the same time in this and other economies.

Consider the fact that, even in a period of stable economic activity, some workers enter the labor force for the first time; others enter after a period of nonparticipation; and still others quit or are fired or laid off. These workers seek out job offers. (Note that they do not seek out *jobs,* because anyone can get a job if he or she is willing to accept a low enough wage rate.) When seeking out job offers, unemployed workers have imperfect information about present wage rates and future wage rates. However, the information they do have gives them some idea. With this information, unemployed workers seek out jobs on the basis of a **reservation wage rate,** below which they will not accept a job offer. That reservation wage rate is a function of the wages they might have had during their last job and the wages they think their former fellow employees are now receiving. Even in a situation of equilibrium where the economy—that is, aggregate demand—is steadily growing, unemployed workers will set reservation wages at such a level that they do not immediately get a job; to do otherwise would probably mean that they might set too low a wage rate or accept too "undesirable" a job and would, thereby, suffer a reduction in their lifetime earnings. Thus, even in a period of stable economic activity, there will be some unemployment due to the lack of perfect information on the part of employees and, indeed, on the part of employers. This is called normal or **frictional unemployment.**

Now consider a situation in which the economy has a steady annual inflation rate of, say, ten percent. This steady inflation rate is included in all the wage expectations of both employers and employees in the economy. Thus, any prospective employee will add a ten-percent inflation rate to his or her reservation wage. With such steady-state inflation, businesses are willing to include a ten-percent inflationary premium in wages because they know that each year they can raise their prices by ten percent and sell the predicted number of goods.

What will happen if the growth rate of aggregate demand slows from a ten-percent inflation rate to a five-percent rate? In other words, given the growth rate of private plus government demand, suppose that, in the long run, prices must rise at five percent a year. No one, however, has perfect information about this reduction in the growth rate in aggregate demand. Workers will continue to demand wage increases that include a ten-percent inflationary premium. In the beginning, employers will grant those wage increases because they, too, lack information about the reduction in the growth rate of the economy. However, because the growth rate in aggregate demand has slowed down, some businesses will not sell as many goods as they anticipated at the prices they had been setting. They will find that their inventories are rising. To reduce unwanted inventories, they will reduce production and output.

Reduced production and output will reduce the demand for employees. Some employees will be laid off; others, who would have been hired had nothing changed, will not be. However, workers' reservation-wage demands do not immediately respond to this increase in the unemployment rate. Why? Because they do not have information that the increase in unemployment is other than a passing event. Or they expect the cause of the slackening demand to be eliminated as soon as the government panics at the increase in unemployment. They will continue to include the ten-percent inflationary premium in their wage demands. That means that unemployed workers will remain unemployed longer. Because the average duration of unemployment will rise, so will the rate of unemployment. Thus, we see that stagflation can be caused simply by the lack of information in the labor market. The growth rate in aggregate demand has slowed (whether because of a reduced growth rate of the money supply, or a contractionary fiscal policy, or a change in business expectations about the future profitability of investment). Prices will continue to rise, inventories will continue to increase above their optimal levels, and the unemployment rate will continue to rise for a time. In a sense, then, the expectation of a continued rise in prices leads to higher prices. This is the so-called wage-price spiral. Sooner or later, this wage-price spiral must dwindle as unemployment grows to critical levels. Workers eventually get the message and reduce their reservation wage rate; employers eventually refuse to grant ever-increasing wages. We do not expect the price level to start falling, however; we expect that the rate of increase in prices will fall so that, eventually, the equilibrium rate of inflation will drop to five percent a year.

Periods of stagflation or slumpflation do not defy economic analysis and do not signify that the economy is not working as it did formerly. They are merely periods during which the growth rate of aggregate demand has slowed from some previous higher level, in a world of imperfect information.

Summary

Stagflation occurs when prices continue to rise in the face of a recession. Cost-push market-power theories that attempt to explain stagflation do not predict very well. The notion that the Phillips curve trade-off between the rate of unemployment and the rate of inflation has worsened is also an inadequate explanation of stagflation. An alternative explanation involves imperfect information in labor markets. When monetary and fiscal policies or business expectations are no longer consistent with the same rate of growth in aggregate demand that everyone became used to, workers and businesses will require time to adjust because of imperfect information. The average duration of unemployment will increase until workers and businesses learn that there has been a permanent reduction in the rate of growth of aggregate demand. This is why we can see continued rising prices along with rising unemployment.

Discussion Questions

1. Why do expectations play such an important part in explaining stagflation?

2. What does it mean to say that the Phillips curve trade-off has worsened in recent years?

Short-Run Stabilization Policies— Fact or Fiction?

Key Terms

short-run stabilization policy Attempts by the federal government to influence changes in the rate of growth of aggregate demand in the short run to iron out the ups and downs in overall business activity.

econometric forecasting models Models of how the economy works derived from combining economic theory with mathematics and statistics.

information or recognition lag The time between when an economic phenomenon occurs and when it is recognized.

action lag The time between when an economic phenomenon is recognized and when some policy change goes into effect.

effect lag The time between when a policy change has been made and when the results are felt in the economy.

macroeconomic models Models of how the entire economy works and from which predictions of future rates of inflation, rates of unemployment, and the like can be calculated.

income surtax A tax added onto the existing income tax.

In the 1960s, many economists began to talk about the death of the business cycle. Today no such notion is ever discussed because the business cycle is indeed still with us. Government policy makers, however, see it as their job to reduce as much as possible the extreme ups and downs in that business cycle. This is the goal of what is called **short-run stabilization policy.**

Short-run stabilization policy was unheard of prior to the Great Depression for two main reasons. First, it was then the consensus among economists that the economy was self-regulating. Second, the importance of fiscal policy didn't really gain a foothold until after the publication of Keyne's *General Theory* (1936).

By the end of World War II, Congress made explicit the federal government's responsibility to stabilize economic activity in the short run. The Employment Act of 1946 declared, among other things, that the federal government is responsible for promoting "maximum" employment, production, and purchasing power sufficient to guarantee that the ups and downs in economic activity will be smoothed out. Maximum employment has been taken to mean full employment, but, as we saw in chapter 9, the definition of full employment is arbitrary. Thus, policy makers have the problem of deciding when they should engage in active expansionary policies to promote full employment.

Let's assume there is no problem of defining full employment and ask the question, "When does the policy maker decide that an appropriately expansionary or contractionary monetary and/or fiscal policy should be put into effect?" The decision is generally based on a mixture of information about the current economic scene; this includes estimates of the current rate of inflation, the current rate of unemployment, the current level of new business capital formation, and so on. Additionally, predictions about future economic activity, based on current and past data, must be included. These predictions are obtainable from myriad **econometric forecasting models.** Although policy makers are well aware of the problems inherent in model building, they must rely on formal predictions about the future as well as on seat-of-the-pants "guesstimate" predictions. Any model used has to rely on the available information. And the available information about the current state of the economy may not be very accurate and won't, therefore, yield accurate predictions about the future.

For any short-run stabilization policy making, three time lags must always be taken into account: First (one we just mentioned), the **information or recognition lag;** second, the **action lag;** and, third, the **effect lag.** For any policy to be made, information about the state of the economy must be known. However, we do not know precisely what is happening concurrently to capital formation, unemployment, changes in prices, and so on. We only know after the fact and with a lag— the information lag. The size of this lag is crucially dependent on how quickly accurate information can be obtained, but accurate information about the entire economy sometimes doesn't come for months. In other words, we might not recognize that we are in a recession until six months after it starts. This is often called the recognition lag for monetary and fiscal policy. If this lag isn't a big enough problem, another one awaits policy makers, particularly with respect to fiscal policy.

Once it is discovered that, for example, we are indeed in a recession, a long period—the action lag—can elapse before any policy is put into effect. This is particularly true of tax cuts or increases meant to stabilize the economy. In 1961 the Kennedy administration suggested a tax cut. It didn't pass until 1964, a lag of three years. Monetary policy does not suffer from the same action lag because the Board of Governors of the Federal Reserve System meets thirteen times a year and can almost instantaneously put into effect any policy it decides upon. All the Federal Reserve must do is instruct the trading desk at the New York Fed how to proceed. In sum, then, the action lag can be long and variable for fiscal policy, but it will generally be relatively short for monetary policy.

Even if there were no recognition or information lag and no action lag, there would still be an effect lag because even a perfect economic policy change will not have an immediate impact upon the economy. The effects of increased government spending take time to work. The same problem arises with a change in taxes. A change in the growth rate in the money supply may not have an effect for several months or several years. Some economists say that for fiscal policy the effect lag can be distributed over a period of several years. Some researchers contend that, although the lag in monetary policy may be only six months, it can also drag out over a period of several years. In any event, all agree that there is great variability in the length of effect lags.

Now you can see the problems inherent in trying to stabilize the economy in the short run. Assume you are a policy maker, and you have just discovered that the economy is in a recession. You try to get taxes changed to counter that recession. What kind of problems will you encounter? First, we may have already been in a recession for six months or one year before it was realized. Second, it may take another year or two for Congress to put the tax package change into force. And, third, it may take still another year before the full effect of that fiscal policy change is felt in the economy. By that time, however, the economy may have already turned around and entered an upswing. The fiscal policy change will then be inappropriate and only add fuel to an already existing inflation.

The long and variable lags involved in short-run stabilization policy have prompted some critics of such policies to recommend essentially no short-run stabilization attempts at all, both from a monetary and a fiscal policy point of view. The most outspoken proponent of stable—that is, nondiscretionary—monetary policy is Milton Friedman, formerly of the University of Chicago. For many years, Friedman has been a proponent of the so-called monetary rule (discussed in chapter 24), which would allow the money supply to grow at a fixed rate over a period of one year. This rate could not be altered by the Federal Open Market Committee; in fact, that committee would have no function if a monetary rule were instituted.

In fiscal policy, there are numerous advocates of a long-run commitment to a balanced full-employment budget. Essentially, then, discretionary fiscal policy would not be used as a tool to change the direction of economic activity in the short run. Perhaps you can see that the adoption of a monetary rule and a long-run commitment to a balanced full-employment federal budget would, to a large extent, eliminate the necessity of developing and using **macroeconomic models** as part of the base on which short-run stabilization policies are formed.

Since stabilization policy can be based on fiscal as well as monetary tools, problems of coordination are possible. What if the fiscal authorities—the president and Congress—decide on one policy, and the monetary authorities—the Fed—decide on another? As a matter of fact, policies have conflicted at times in the past. For example, in 1968 a fiscal policy of restraint was adopted by Congress in the form of a temporary **income surtax.** However, soon after that surtax went into effect, the monetary authorities engaged in what would have to be considered an expansionary policy by increasing the rate of growth of the money supply. It would seem that unless all policy making were put under one roof, so to speak, the problem of coordination sometimes could be serious enough to negate policies that might otherwise help stabilize our economy.

A relatively new school of macroeconomic thought is developing that, if it is correct, has serious repercussions for policy making. According to this school, the debate between the effectiveness of monetary versus fiscal policy is irrelevant. The argument is as follows: The only way short-run stabilization policy can work is by the public being temporarily fooled; if the public knew exactly what was going to happen, it would be able to capitalize on that information and effectively negate it.[1] This is similar to the argument that information about a company

---

[1]Economists call this the theory of rational expectations.

is useless for an investor wishing to invest in that company because the information, if accurate, will already have been used by someone else, and the current price of the company's stock will reflect the information. If we look specifically at the trade-off in the Phillips curve, we can apply the same argument: The employment effect depicted in the Phillips curve results from fooling individuals about the future rate of inflation.

If the same argument can be used for the economy as a whole, then government policy makers can succeed only to the extent that they fool the public. However, you can't fool all the people all the time. Thus, the public will eventually catch on to what government policy makers are doing, and a new policy will have to be devised to have any effect. We would even extend this analysis to its ultimate conclusion; that is, even if policy makers use extremely complicated econometric models to make predictions on which to base their policies, economic agents in our society will eventually find it profitable to figure out these models so they won't be fooled. The models then become useless as a prediction device, no matter how many equations are involved or how long the computer works on them.

Such a view of our economy is indeed disconcerting to those who believe that doing something is better than doing nothing. According to these critics, however, long-run stable monetary and fiscal policies such as those just mentioned—a monetary rule and a long-run, balanced, full-employment budget—really involve "doing nothing." If it's true that it's impossible to stabilize in the future, then we may be better off by not making any attempt at all, because we would not then exacerbate the ups and downs in business activity.

Summary

Short-run stabilization policy may be difficult because of the time lags involved in recognizing when a new policy should be put into effect, of putting that new policy into effect, and of having that new policy take effect. The existence of long and variable lags have prompted critics to argue in favor of a monetary rule and a commitment to a balanced full-employment budget. Even if such lags did not exist, there are often conflicts between the monetary and fiscal authorities: one group may decide to tighten up while the other group decides to loosen up. Perhaps the debate about which policy to use, whether it be monetary or fiscal, is beside the point if, in fact, people in the economy learn quickly about the effects of any short-run stabilization policy. In other words, if expectations are rational, then short-run stabilization policies can only succeed as long as they fool people.

Discussion Questions

1. Why do we say that the Phillips curve trade-off only exists as long as workers are fooled?

2. What does it mean to say that information about the future profitability of a company is already included in the current price of that company's stock?

The
Political-Business
Cycle

Key Terms

short-run Phillips curve The trade-off that exists between unemployment and inflation over a short period of time, say a year.
long-run Phillips curve The trade-off that exists between unemployment and inflation over a long period of time, say several years.

Do politicians have an incentive to cause ups and downs in economic activity? Do they have an incentive to maintain an ongoing inflation? A number of economists say they do. Let's discuss the second question first.

In several earlier chapters we saw that the rate of inflation was an important determinant of the share of national income going to government because of our progressive income tax system. That is, because we have a progressive income tax system, rises in nominal income force individual taxpayers into ever-higher marginal tax brackets. Thus, even if taxpayers' real income does not rise, the amount of income that goes to government will rise. For example, a person who gets a ten-percent raise that just matches a ten-percent rise in prices will undoubtedly end up with less take-home pay because that person will probably be pushed into a higher marginal tax bracket,

166

thus raising his or her overall effective tax rate. Tax rates are generally legislated by Congress. One way for Congress to obtain an ever-increasing share of real output of the economy without legislation is by causing inflation, thus creating the situation just described. Hence, strange as this notion may seem, governments do have an incentive to maintain an inflation.

What about the idea that politicians cause the business cycle? This notion has been put forward by an economist at Yale, William Nordhaus. If American politicians think the unemployment rate should be around six percent and anything above that is politically disastrous, they will want to engage in expansionary fiscal policies prior to elections to drive down the unemployment rate. As pointed out in chapter 26, it is certainly possible to reduce the unemployment rate, particularly in the short run, without any adverse inflationary effects, because short-run effects of expansionary aggregate demand policies are primarily on output rather than on prices. A **short-run Phillips curve** does exist, and it is much more favorable, particularly to a politician, than the **long-run Phillips curve** trade-off. So, the politician times the economic stimulus to occur just before the election and postpones the full inflationary impact until after the election. The government then switches to an anti-inflationary policy, which produces a recession about one year after the election. Nordhaus indicates that the data support his hypothesis: The unemployment rate was relatively low in 1948, 1952, 1956, 1968, and 1972. And in each of these years, recessions followed the presidential elections, either immediately or within eight to thirteen months.

If we look at the period from 1947 through 1976, we find that inflation and unemployment rates declined simultaneously during only six of those years. Not surprisingly, there was a presidential election during four of those six years. The data show that inflation and unemployment rates simultaneously declined fifty percent of the time during presidential election years but less than ten percent of the time during other years.

In all fairness to historical accuracy, we must point out that the 1960 election was an exception to Nordhaus's thesis. There was a recession during that year, and John F. Kennedy used this fact in his campaign when he promised to "get this country moving again."

Looking at what happened during the Ford administration, we find that the political-business cycle hypothesis predicted quite well. The 1975 tax cut and aggressively expansionary fiscal policy on the part of Congress and the president presumably was passed in an attempt to lower the unemployment rate by the time of the political campaigns in 1976. By mid-1977, the price level had started to rise at a more rapid rate than during the previous year. In 1978, it hit 9.3 percent and went even higher in 1979. Nordhaus's theory predicted well.

However, it is possible that the political-business cycle may be coming to a close if, in fact, the political climate is changing. Perhaps the public is no longer willing to accept inflation, or it may better understand the role of incumbent politicians in causing it. In other words, the public's fear of inflation may now outweigh its fear of unemployment. Thus, temporarily high unemployment rates may be politically more acceptable in the future than a high rate of inflation. Avoiding unemployment at all costs may no longer be appropriate.

Looking at our political situation, we presumably have a democracy where a majority coalition determines public policy. Thus, even if the minority is disadvantaged by temporarily high unemployment rates, the majority may feel it is better off with anti-inflationary aggregate demand policies of Congress and the president. This may be particularly true as more and more individuals have less trouble dealing with unemployment because they get relatively high unemployment compensation benefits. Clearly, the Reagan administration believed that getting rid of inflation was more important than worrying about rising unemployment. By the summer of 1982, the unemployment rate had hit almost ten percent, but the rate of inflation had fallen to historically very low levels.

It is also interesting to speculate that the political-business cycle theory contends that politicians can forever fool the public. Eventually, however, the public should learn that expansionary fiscal policies prior to elections will only temporarily lower the unemployment rate at the expense of higher rates of inflation in the future. Once the public learns this, politicians will be less able to campaign on such a platform.

Summary

Politicians benefit from inflation because of taxflation. In the short run, politicians, especially incumbent presidents, can benefit from inflation caused by expansionary fiscal policies just prior to an election, because those expansionary fiscal policies will reduce unemployment. In general, incumbents have been elected when unemployment has been low during a presidential election year. The political-business cycle therefore involves expansionary fiscal policy prior to the election with anti-inflationary monetary policy after the election. When the public learns this, however, the political-business cycle will no longer work, or even be tried for that matter.

Discussion Questions

1. When Carter lost his bid for reelection, the rate of inflation was rising as was the rate of unemployment. What do you think happened?

2. What would determine which issue—unemployment or inflation—was the most important political issue of the day?

Can Supply Side Economics Work?

Key Terms

supply side economics The school of economic thought in which individuals respond to incentives and therefore will work harder, save more, and invest more if after-tax rates of return to those activities increase.

Laffer curve A curve showing the relationship between a tax rate and total tax revenues raised by that tax. At a zero or 100-percent tax rate, no tax revenues are raised. At some intermediate tax rate, revenues reach a maximum.

Although perhaps already suffering from an early death, **supply side economics** is still occasionally in the news. President Reagan was elected in 1980 to a large extent on a platform that included the notion that reductions in tax rates can increase productivity, income, output, employment, and saving. Some of his supporters went so far as to argue that a reduction in tax rates could even lead to an *increase* in total federal tax revenues. Now that's a true sleight of hand.

You have already been introduced to the notion of incentives in chapter 2 when we talked about the underground economy. You were further introduced to the concept of incentives, marginal tax rates, and loopholes in chapter 3. Briefly, the higher the marginal tax rate, the greater the incentive to find ways not to pay taxes, either through legal tax avoidance, illegal tax evasion (such as joining the underground economy), or less work, saving, and investment. By now everyone knows that this simple proposition dating back perhaps several thousand years was reborn as the **Laffer curve.** Professor of economics Arthur Laffer of the University of Southern California apparently sketched the relationship between marginal tax rates and total tax revenues on a napkin during a lunch with an inquisitive reporter. The Laffer curve is nothing more than a statement that people do respond to incentives. As marginal tax rates get higher and higher, people start figuring more and more ways to avoid taxes and indeed some people start working less, taking longer vacations, retiring earlier, and so on.

Not surprisingly, at some rate, an increase in the marginal tax rate will lead to a reduction in total tax revenues rather than an increase. Why? Simply because at some high marginal tax rate any further increases will backfire in the sense that they will cause an overreaction by taxpayers. That overreaction will consist of more than the usual attempts to avoid and evade taxes owed to the federal government.

Of course, as a theoretical proposition (or perhaps even as a truism) the Laffer curve cannot be denied. Rather, the question that becomes important is, Where are we on the Laffer curve? Are marginal tax rates so high in the United States that we are past the point of the federal government imposing a maximum tax collection? If so, then the extreme supply side version of the Laffer curve is correct—a reduction in marginal tax rates will lead to an *increase* in total tax revenues. It is one thing to *hope* that the United States is actually in such a situation so that tax rate reductions will not create larger federal government deficits. It is quite another thing for that hope to be a reality.

At the time that President Reagan pushed through his so-called monumental tax cut in 1981, there was precious little research to show that a tax rate cut would lead to a tax revenue increase. Some research done, however, showed that secondary workers such as women and teenagers are more responsive to changes in tax rate than are prime age males. It has been estimated that a 1-percent increase in after-tax income will lead to a .9-percent increase in hours worked by adult women, but only a .15-percent increase in work effort for the overall work force. Other research has indicated that over the last twenty years, increases in income and payroll taxes have reduced the labor supply of married males by 8 percent and of married females by almost 30 percent.

Little work has been done to predict how much of the underground economy will come above ground if marginal tax rates are reduced below what they are today. Of course we know that *some* underground economic activity will start being reported as marginal tax rates fall. People do respond to incentives. The big question is, of course, By how much? The same is true for investment behavior. Certainly if the after-tax rate of return to investment increases, more investment will be undertaken. But again, How much? Supply siders have just begun detailed research to demonstrate the empirically predicted effects of reductions in marginal tax rates on underground versus reported activity, and on investment activity.

Perhaps a more rational and less histrionic approach to supply side predictions can be found. While it may be simply wishful thinking that in the immediate future a tax rate cut will increase federal government revenues, it may not be just fanciful for the long run. The argument goes as follows: A reduction in marginal tax rates today may lead to increased federal budget deficits today. But, if properly structured, reductions in marginal tax rates will increase economic growth by increasing labor force participation, work effort, saving, and investment. Eventually, this increased economic growth will cause the "pie" to grow so much that even at the lower marginal tax rates, the federal government will collect more total tax revenues.

No sooner was the ink dried on Reagan's tax cut legislation in 1981 than critics pointed out that "it" was not working. Supply side economics quickly fell into disrepute because the economy did not immediately pull out of its recession as the more vocal of these critics predicted. And federal government deficits soon reached the $100-billion mark. Dispassionate analysis of what the Tax Reduction Act of 1981 really did shows, however, that supply side economics was never really given a chance. The so-called tax cut package of 1981 was merely a reduction in tax *increases* that would have occurred in its absence. Look at the data in Table 29–1. The average American's average tax rate will be slightly higher in 1984 than in 1980.

In other words, the tax bite by the federal government stayed about the same. Supply side economics requires that tax rates fall, not stay the same. But, you may be asking, how could tax rates remain the same when marginal tax rates were to be cut by twenty-five percent over a three-year period? The answer has to do with scheduled increases in Social Security taxes and bracket creep, or taxflation, a subject we have already discussed. Inflation will continue to push individuals into higher and higher tax brackets. (In 1985, unless Congress changes its mind, tax brackets will be indexed to the rate of inflation so

TABLE 29.1

Income Class in 1980	1980		1984	
	After-tax purchasing power	Average tax rate	After-tax purchasing power (1980 $s)	Average tax rate
Low income ($15,000)	$12,327	17.8%	$12,084	19.4%
Median income ($24,000)	$18,129	24.5%	$17,978	25.1%
High income ($45,000)	$30,104	33.0%	$29,420	34.6%

that in principle bracket creep will disappear.) The press may have hailed the 1981 tax cut as the largest ever, but effectively it is not turning out that way.

Summary

Supply side economics involve the simple proposition that work effort, investment effort, and the like respond positively to increases in after-tax rates of return. In other words, individuals respond to incentives. Because at high marginal tax rates it pays to reduce work effort and to find ways illegally and legally to avoid taxes, after some point, an increase in marginal tax rates will lead to a reduction in total tax revenues. An economy with very high marginal tax rates will witness an increase in total tax revenues when marginal tax rates are reduced. It is an empirical proposition, however, as to where the United States is on this so-called Laffer curve. The tax cuts initiated in 1981 ultimately will not prove or disprove the effectiveness of supply side economics. Because of bracket creep and Social Security tax increases, the average American will be paying about the same in taxes in 1985 as he or she paid in 1981.

Discussion Questions

1. Beginning economics students learn that supply curves are upward sloping. What does this have to do with supply side economics and the Laffer curve?

2. Why is the word *marginal* inserted before tax rate throughout this chapter?

3. Why will indexation of the federal income tax system in 1985 eliminate the problem of bracket creep?

PART SEVEN

International
Trade
and
finance

The Cost of Trade Restrictions

Key Terms

tariffs Taxes levied specifically on imports.

import quotas A quantity restriction on the amount of imports of a specific good that can be brought into a country.

embargo A government-imposed restriction on the movement of goods.

import surcharge A tariff levied on the basis of existing tariffs.

Mark Twain was rumored to have once said that the free traders win all the arguments, but the protectionists win all the votes. Protectionism has been steadily on the increase, not only in the form of **tariffs** but also in the form of **import quotas,** export restrictions, and quality restrictions on imports.

The issue of restricting imports came to the fore in the 1980s when Japanese automobiles and steel seemed to be taking away American jobs. The argument in favor of restricting imports from Japan went as follows: The Japanese are too "competitive" with the United States. Their automobile manufacturers and steel producers are destroying American jobs in automobiles and steel. Thus, Americans are being hurt by Japanese competition. What should we do? The answer seems obvious: Re-

177

strict imports any way possible, either voluntarily by the Japanese government, by charging higher tariffs, or by using quotas.

The argument in favor of restricting imports is incomplete, however. We must remember that the only way the United States ultimately pays for its imports is by exporting goods and services. In other words, we may seemingly be paying for imports with dollars, but what good are those dollars to foreigners? The dollars are only good if they are eventually exchanged for American goods and services. After all, Japanese importers do not pay their workers in dollars—they must pay them in yen.

The fact of the matter is that *imports are paid for by exports.* That simple truism means that whenever we restrict imports, we thereby restrict exports. Although it seems anomalous, it is true nonetheless. Imports and exports, in the long run, must be equal in value. Therefore, whenever we import something (as opposed to purchasing it domestically) while we may be losing jobs in the import-competing industry, we will be gaining jobs in the export industry; foreigners use the dollars earned from the goods that we import to purchase our exports.

Historically, when imports increase as a percentage of gross national product so, too, do exports. For example, in 1976 U.S. imports represented 7.3 percent of GNP and U.S. exports represented 6.7 percent. By June 30, 1980 U.S. imports had risen to 11.2 percent of GNP. U.S. exports had also increased to almost 10 percent of GNP. As imports have increased so, too, have exports. This has been true for every other country in the world. Indeed, it would be impossible for things to be otherwise.

Now consider one of the ways of restricting imports—a quota system. Under the quota system, countries are limited to a specified amount of trade. Consider a restriction on the import of automobiles. In the absence of world trade, the domestic (U.S.) prices will be determined by the interaction of domestic demand and supply. When world trade opens up,

Americans will buy domestically produced and foreign produced automobiles. A quota, however, limits the amount of automobiles that can be imported, thereby reducing the supply to U.S. consumers. As a result, U.S. consumers pay higher prices; domestic automobile and steel manufacturers sell more (and foreign manufacturers sell less) than they would have without the import restrictions on autos.

The beneficiaries are clearly workers in American automobile and steel industries, as well as stockholders in those industries. But as we pointed out above, imports are paid for by exports. Although a restriction on imports would increase jobs in the import-competing industry, it would reduce jobs in all export industries. U.S. automobile and steel workers would benefit at the expense of workers in export industries.

Interestingly, at the beginning of this decade workers in domestic automobile and steel manufacturing were averaging between $10.50 and $12.00 an hour, whereas the average for all private, nonagricultural workers was less than $7.00 an hour. A restriction on automobile imports would have the effect of benefiting higher-paid workers at the expense of lower-paid workers.

Additionally, any restriction on Japanese auto imports hurts domestic consumers because it denies them the ability, or at least the choice, of purchasing automobiles at lower prices than would otherwise be available. While it reduces consumers' alternatives, it simultaneously reduces the competitive pressures on American automobile manufacturers to produce autos that compare favorably with cars made in Japan.

Another way to restrict trade between countries is by imposing a tax on imported products. The tax, called a tariff, is imposed so that no similar tax is applied to identical products produced domestically.

A U.S. imposed tariff on an import raises the price of the product, produced by both foreign and domestic producers, to United States residents. Purchasers of imported goods must now pay the world price plus the tariff. They cannot get foreign goods any cheaper because everyone must pay the tariff. On domestically produced and sold import-competing goods, the U.S. Treasury does not impose a tariff, so the producers get to keep all of the revenues. Since the sale price of import-competing goods is higher with than without the tariff, domestic producers are willing to increase the output of them. On the other hand, consumers will buy less at the higher price that now faces them. This decrease in imports is similar to the one we discussed with a quota system; however, there are differences.

In both cases, the price is higher and the quantity of imports falls. The big difference is that with the quota system, no government revenues (taxes) were collected. With the tariff system, the government keeps the tariff, and these revenues can be used to reduce taxes or to increase government expenditures. Again, the workers and stockholders in the domestic import-competing industries benefit at the expense of workers in the export industries.

International trade has been stifled in other ways also. For example, on June 28, 1973, the Nixon administration abruptly placed an **embargo** on U.S. soybean exports. Without warning, the major supply of one of Japan's basic foodstufffs was virtually cut off. All of the managing directors of Japanese soybean processing firms had to go elsewhere to find soybeans, and they had to act quickly. They went to Brazil, for example. The embargo did not last for long, but its long-run effects are still being felt. Because of the U.S. embargo on soybean exports, Brazil has become a major world soybean supplier. Before the U.S. embargo, Brazil had accounted for only eighteen percent of world soybean sales, whereas the U.S. commanded eighty percent. Today Brazil has forty percent of this market, while the U.S. share has shrunk to thirty-five percent.

The soybean embargo lasted only a few weeks, but its impact has lasted for more than a decade. The supposed reasoning behind the soybean export restriction was to cut off some of the foreign demand for domestic soybeans so as to keep their prices from rising. Some analysts have estimated that the cost of the soybean export freeze has been tens of billions of dollars of lost export sales.

The soybean export freeze was just part of a never-ending set of restrictions on foreign trade. Consider that we had, in 1971, a ten-percent across-the-board **import surcharge,** a freeze on iron and steel imports in 1972, beef quotas in 1974, a freeze on grain sales to the Soviet Union in 1975 and again in 1978, a limitation on export sales to countries violating "human rights" in 1978, and, finally, a freeze on all Iranian assets held in the United States in 1979.

In all cases, these restrictions on international trade seem to make sense and were done for "good" reasons. But in all cases, the long-run effect has been to reduce the amount of international trade, particularly that emanating to and from the United States. Estimates of the domestic costs of the grain embargo in 1980–81 are astounding— $11.5 billion in lost output, 310,000 jobs lost, and a reduction of $3.1 billion in personal income, plus several billion dollars in direct government costs.

Politicians will discharge with much of the above analysis, nonetheless. John Connally, the architect of the 1971 import surcharge under Nixon, has argued that the United States should use its economic clout even more frequently to pursue its national interests. When queried about the long-run effects of the soybean embargo and the fact that the Japanese are now buying more from Brazil than from us, Connally stated, "they would go buy somewhere else on the basis of price anyway."

Summary

Imports are paid by exports. Therefore, any restriction on imports ultimately leads to a reduction in the amount of exports sold. Nonetheless, there are numerous restrictions on international trade. Under a quota system, certain countries are allowed to export to the United States only specified quantities of a particular good per year. Workers and stockhholders in the domestic import-competing industries benefit; consumers of the goods that are put under quota lose. Quotas also reduce the competitiveness of domestic production because they eliminate potential competition from abroad. Another way to restrict imports is through tariffs. They have a similar effect to quotas except the federal government collects import duties. In both cases, the price of domestically produced import-competing goods rises. Numerous other attempts at stifling international trade have occurred. In the long run, they have led to less trade for the United States.

Discussion Questions

1. What does it mean to say that imports are paid for by exports?

2. Certain goods are fungible. That is, one unit cannot be distinguished from another unit. Wheat is one of them. If the United States refuses to sell wheat to the Soviet Union, will this ultimately affect the amount of wheat that the Soviet Union ends up buying in world markets?

Currency Speculation

Key Terms

foreign exchange market The market in which the world's currencies are traded.

spot market The market for current buying and selling of a commodity—in this case, foreign exchange. In other words, the market for purchase and sale of foreign exchange today for delivery today.

forward market The market for buying and selling commodities for delivery at a later date.

going long Actually owning a commodity.

going short Being in a position where you have agreed to sell something at a future date.

hedging The process of reducing future risk by simultaneously going long and short for a specific commodity—in this case, foreign exchange.

fixed exchange rates A system of exchange rates in which governments arbitrarily fix the foreign exchange rate of their currency and are willing to step in to foreign exchange markets to keep that exchange rate fixed.

devalue Under a fixed exchange rate system, to reduce unilaterally the foreign exchange value of a country's currency.

revalue Under a fixed exchange rate system, to increase arbitrarily the foreign exchange rate value of a country's currency done by that country's government.

floating exchange rates A system in which the foreign exchange rate is determined completely by the unrestricted forces of supply and demand in the foreign exchange market.

183

futures market Similar to a forward market but one in which specified commodities of a specified quality and quantity are traded in a more organized way. There exists a futures market in foreign exchange for certain currencies.

Foreign currency is an asset, just like domestic currency, stocks, bonds, and houses. Many investors decide to hold foreign currency as one of the assets in their portfolio. Their actions, however, can cause pressures on foreign exchange rates, thereby creating problems in international trade. Let's take a look at the **foreign exchange market,** who is in it, and how it affects exchange rates and trade.

Many individuals and institutions participate in the foreign exchange market, just as many different types of people and institutions are interested in other types of assets, such as stocks and bonds. Thus, we expect to see and do see commercial banks, corporations, businesspersons, doctors, lawyers, and sheiks from the Middle East participating in the foreign exchange market. Major banks and individual foreign exchange currency specialists are, however, the leading participants in the field.

We have referred several times now to the foreign exchange market. This is the money center through which the world's leading currencies are bought and sold. It involves a network of currency trading departments at the world's major banks. This interbank system deals mainly with transactions of $1 million or more at a time. In addition, there is the International Monetary Market, an organized exchange in which currencies are traded. Smaller corporations and individuals usually deal through the International Monetary Market.

In order to understand how the foreign exchange market works and why people would trade different currencies, we must look at the two different types of markets—one for buying and selling currencies today, called the **spot market,** and the other for buying and selling currencies in the future, called the **forward market.**

Let's assume that you are an investor who thinks that the German mark is going to go up in value in the near future. You can exchange dollars in the foreign exchange market for German marks. You do this in the spot market, either through an international currency department at a major bank, the International Monetary Fund, or various smaller, independent currency dealers. We say that you have **gone long** in German marks—that is, you own them and expect their price to rise in the future. Now, if you owned German marks already and felt that their value was going to fall in terms of dollars, you might take your German marks to one of the places just mentioned and sell them; you sell them because of an anticipated decrease in their value.

In essence, then, the spot currency market is no different than the stock market, for example. The buying and selling of stocks are done on the basis of people's expectations of future prices of those stocks. The buying and selling of currency by investors also involves different anticipations of the future price of those currencies. Additionally, firms and individuals making international transactions—engaging in international trade—will utilize the spot currency market for those transactions. No investment activities are undertaken in such a case. If, say, Lockheed needed to obtain $1 million worth of British pounds in order to pay for the delivery of a Rolls Royce jet engine, it would go to the foreign exchange market to purchase those pounds in order to make the payment.

Agreements to buy and sell currencies in the future at prices specified today are the basis of the forward exchange market. Forward contracts are issued in which the seller of the contract agrees to deliver a specified amount of some foreign currency for a specified price at a specified future date. The buyer of the forward contract promises to pay for it on that date. We say that the seller of the contract has **gone short,** or has a "short position" in the foreign exchange (assuming that he or she doesn't own the currency already): He or she agrees to deliver it for sale. The buyer of the contract has gone long, or has a "long position" in the foreign exchange; he or she has agreed to buy foreign currency later.

Let's take a specific example involving an American farmer selling corn to West Germany. There are several steps in the process.

1. The farmer agrees to send one million bushels of corn to a German buyer in exchange for 2 million German marks in six months. The farmer, though, does not know what 2 million German marks will be worth in U.S. dollars in half a year. Therefore, the farmer attempts to protect himself or herself from the risk of German marks falling in value relative to the dollar.

2. In order to protect himself or herself, the farmer sells a forward contract to a U.S. bank in which the farmer agrees to deliver 2 million German marks in six months in exchange for, say, $1 million at that time. The bank accepting the forward contract is estimating that the exchange in six months will be one dollar for two German marks.

3. Six months later, the American farmer delivers the corn to the German buyer and is paid the 2 million marks. The farmer takes the marks to the U.S. bank and receives $1 million as promised.

In this situation, the farmer was **hedging** the risk inherent in making a contract to receive foreign currency at a later date. The bank took over that risk. If the value of the German mark fell in six months, the bank would suffer the loss. On the other hand, if the value of the German mark increased in six months, the bank would receive the gain. In other words, by transferring the risk to the bank, the farmer gives up the possibility of earning more than he or she bargained for with the German buyer of corn.

It is often argued that speculators (as opposed to hedgers, such as our American farmer) cause disruptions in the international currency foreign exchange market and, therefore, disruptions in international trade. We have just seen, that the existence of a forward market in foreign currency allows exporters and importers to specialize in the selling and buying of items in international trade. The ability of manufacturers in each country to protect themselves from risk exposure through foreign exchange fluctuations undoubtedly promotes international trade. Thus, the existence of a forward contract market in foreign exchange would appear to benefit all nations to the extent that it promotes more trade.

What about the possibility of speculators, both in the spot and forward markets, exaggerating fluctuations in exchange rates? This possibility certainly exists, as it does in all asset markets, including the stock market, the commodities market, the bond market, and the real estate market. It can be argued that, under a system of **fixed exchange rates** (or, more correctly, a system of occasionally adjusted fixed exchange rates), speculators can (and indeed did in the past) cause currency crises. After all, in many situations such speculation had very little risk. Consider an era of fixed exchange rates where the British pound is in a weakened condition—that is, the supply of pounds in the foreign exchange market consistently exceeds the demand for pounds. Only intervention by British and foreign central banks keeps the pound's value stable. Speculators, reasoning that the British will have to **devalue** the pound (that is, lower its value in foreign exchange), could further put pressure on the pound's value by selling more and more forward contracts. In other words, in anticipation of the lower price of the pound in the future, speculators agree to sell lots of pounds in the future at today's prices. They reason that when the forward contract comes due, they can purchase the pound at a lower price than that at which they agreed to sell it. Furthermore, people living in Britain might wish to speculate under such circumstances by selling many of their pounds for other, presumably stronger, currencies.[1] If the speculators guessed right and the British government was forced to de- value, then the speculators would all gain. If they guessed wrong, the only thing they would lose is the interest on the amount of money they had tied up in the investment. Why? Because, under a fixed exchange rate system, it would be difficult to imagine that the British government would actually increase the value of, or **revalue,** the pound. Thus, in such circum- stances, speculation probably can lead to difficulties in the foreign exchange market.

In a **floating exchange rate** market, however, it is not at all clear that speculation (as opposed to hedging) leads to less stability in foreign exchange rates. After all, speculators are attempting to predict future price changes. They make their predictions based on information about the strength of various economies, monetary policies in various economies, and so on. If they are correct, they will be rewarded by a profit; if they are incorrect, they will lose. To the extent that they are correct, they will cause foreign exchange rates to adjust more quickly to underlying supply-and-demand conditions than they would have otherwise. In a sense, then, speculation leads to a more efficiently working foreign exchange market. At least some studies have shown that the existence of an organized forward market (called a **futures market** for organized exchanges) for commodities has reduced the variability in commodity prices. Presumably, the ability of speculators to buy and sell forward contracts also leads to less variability in exchange rates than would exist otherwise.

---

[1]We assume no British government restrictions.

Summary

Individuals wishing to obtain foreign exchange currently go to the foreign exchange spot market. Individuals wishing to obtain commitments in the future go to the foreign exchange forward market. Individuals and institutions that wish to hedge can simultaneously go short and go long in a foreign currency and therefore are protected from changes in the foreign exchange rate. Under a fixed exchange rate system, speculation can be destabilizing. It is difficult, if not impossible, though, for speculation to be destabilizing under a floating exchange rate system.

Discussion Questions

1. Why does the foreign exchange market exist?

2. What is the difference between the fixed exchange rate system and the floating exchange rate system, and how does this difference impact on the ability of speculators to destabilize the foreign exchange market?

Index

191

†